Ninja Air Fryer Cookbook

150 Amazingly Easy and Delicious Recipes to Fry, Bake, Grill, and Roast with Your Ninja Air Fryer

Melanie Scott

Copyright © 2019 By Melanie Scott All Rights Reserved.

No part of this publication may be reproduced, distributed, or transmitted in any form or by any means, including photocopying, recording, or other electronic or mechanical methods, or by any information storage and retrieval system without the prior written permission of the copyright holder.

Effort has been made to ensure that the information in this book is accurate and complete, however, the author and the publisher do not warrant the accuracy of the information, text and graphics contained within the book due to the rapidly changing nature of science, research, known and unknown facts and internet. The Author and the publisher do not hold any responsibility for errors, omissions or contrary interpretation of the subject matter herein. This book is presented solely for motivational and informational purposes only.

TABLE OF CONTENTS

Introduction 1

Breakfast Recipes 2

    Cheesy Ham Sandwich 2

    Sausage Omelet 2

    Herbed Omelet 3

    Raspberry Pancake 3

    Mozzarella and Egg in a Cup 3

    Tuna Sandwiches 4

    Cheesy Ham Eggplant Boats 4

    Breakfast Sausage Rolls 4

    Italian Sausage Patties 5

    Cheesy Meat Omelet 5

    Delicious Pizza 5

    Herbed Tomatoes Breakfast 6

    Cheesy Onion Omelet 6

    Mediterranean Quiche 6

    Delicious Doughnuts 7

    Egg Rolls 7

    Breakfast Potatoes 8

    Paprika Shirred Eggs 8

    Chicken on Green Bed 8

    Chicken and Spinach Casserole 9

    Bread Pudding 9

    Roasted Peppers Frittata 10

    Cheesy Crispy Straws 10

Poultry Recipes 11

    Delicious Wings 11

    Chicken Kabobs 11

    Fried Whole Chicken 11

    Basil and Cheese Chicken 12

- Chicken Burgers with Avocado ... 12
- Korean Barbecued Satay ... 13
- Buttered Turkey ... 13
- Easy Chicken Thighs ... 13
- Awesome Oregano Chicken Thighs ... 14
- Herbed Chicken ... 14
- Greek Chicken ... 14
- Sweet Chicken Wings ... 15
- Lemon Chicken ... 15
- Asian Chicken ... 15
- Chicken Tenders with Rice ... 16
- Fried Chicken Wings ... 16
- Bleu Chicken ... 17
- Turkey Nuggets ... 17
- Salsa Verde Chicken Breast ... 18
- Chicken Breasts and Veggies ... 18
- Drumsticks ... 18
- Tomato Chicken ... 19
- Soy Sauce Chicken ... 19
- Chicken Thighs ... 19
- Glazed Chicken and Apples ... 20

Meat Recipes ... 21

- Coconut Pork ... 21
- Thai Roasted Beef ... 21
- Greek Style Lamb Chops ... 22
- Beef Shapes ... 22
- Peppercorn Meatloaf Delight ... 22
- Crispiest Roast Pork ... 23
- Beef Kabobs Recipe ... 23
- Philippine Pork Chops ... 24
- Marinated Beef ... 24

- Pork and Shallots ... 24
- French Style Lamb ... 25
- Pork Meatloaf ... 25
- Pork Chops ... 26
- Crunchy Lamb Rack ... 26
- Pork and Bell Peppers ... 27
- Mustard Pork Chops ... 27
- BBQ Pork Ribs ... 27
- Pork Ribs ... 28
- French Beef ... 28
- Smoked Pork Roast ... 28
- Pork and Peanuts ... 29
- Beef Roast ... 29
- Basil Beef Roast ... 29

Fish & Seafood Recipes ... 30

- Parmesan Tilapia ... 30
- Cod and Lime Sauce ... 30
- Salmon and Carrots ... 30
- Chili Salmon Fillets ... 31
- Shrimp and Veggies ... 31
- Tasty Pistachio Crusted Salmon ... 31
- Crab Cakes ... 32
- Cajun Salmon ... 32
- Salmon Fillets ... 32
- Salmon and Orange Vinaigrette ... 33
- Rosemary Shrimp Kabobs ... 33
- Fish Sandwich ... 33
- Fried Salmon ... 34
- Clams and Potatoes ... 34
- Coconut Shrimp ... 34
- Maple Salmon ... 35

Tuna Patties 35

Shrimp and Zucchini 35

Cod Cornflakes Nuggets 36

Sides & Appetizers 37

Creamy Potatoes 37

Steak and Minty Cheese 37

Tomato Bruschetta 37

Parmesan Cabbage Side Dish 38

Herby Fish Skewers 38

Turkey Scotch Eggs 38

Sweet Potato Side Salad 39

Eggplant Chips 39

Pork Bites 39

Melt-in-the-Middle Meatballs 40

Crispy Potato Fries 40

Cauliflower Tater Tots 40

Rosemary Mushrooms 41

Fried Pin Wheels 41

Citrus Cauliflower Mix 42

Zesty Brussels Sprouts with Raisins 42

Italian Mozzarella Sticks 42

Wrapped Asparagus in Bacon 43

Basil and Cilantro Crackers 43

Zucchini Balls 43

Herbed Potatoes 44

French Carrots 44

Cumin Baby Carrots 44

Vegetarian Recipes 45

Quinoa Stuffed Peppers 45

Crispy Nachos 45

Fried Ravioli 45

    Avocado Rolls 46

    Pasta and Roasted Veggies 46

    Prawn Toast 46

    Baby Porcupine Meatballs 47

    Vegetable Tortilla Pizza 47

    Tofu Sandwich 47

    Veggie Skewers 48

    Roasted Vegetable Salad 48

    Asian Style Paneer Cutlet 49

    Crispy Cheese Lings 49

    Sweet Potato Skewers 49

    Delicious Potato Filled Bread Rolls 50

    Pineapple Appetizer Ribs 50

    Crispy Kale Chips 50

    Tomato Stuffed Squash 51

    Cheese Balls 51

Dessert Recipes 52

    Pineapple Cake 52

    Chocolaty Fudge 52

    Passion Fruit Pudding Recipe 53

    Lime Tapioca Pudding 53

    Chocolate Soufflé 53

    Pineapple and Carrot Cake 54

    Fried Doughnuts 54

    Yummy Blueberry Muffins 54

    Chocolate Chip Cookies 55

    Strawberry Cream 55

    Filled Coconut and Oat Cookies 55

    Lime Muffins 56

    Apple Pie 56

    Molten Lava Cake 56

Fried Snickerdoodle Poppers 57

Pumpkin Cake 57

Coffee Cheesecakes Recipe 58

Tangerine Cake Recipe 58

Apple Jam 58

Fried Bananas Recipe 59

Introduction

It is hard to say "No" to your favorite fried snacks and fried cuisines. Fortunately, you do not need to stop consuming them as there is a perfectly healthy way in which you can rip their yummy, crispiness without putting your health at risk

What do you think of the idea of enjoying all the deliciousness of your favorite fried foods without filling your body with harmful fats and calories? The popular and traditional way to prepare fried foods is to submerge them in oil filled frying pan; this method makes foods to soak oils and calories in extremely high amount, which is definitely not a healthy sign for our long-term health

Air Fryer is an ultra-modern kitchen invention that has introduced a revolutionary way of cooking foods by using hot air. It is invented to prepare meals using as much as 80% less amount of oil as compared to traditional method. It is the perfect solution to enjoy crispy foods at home every day.

While we all love having fried-foods, but it comes at a cost of weight gain issues. Less consumption of cooking oil automatically curbs use of calories and promotes the process of fat burning. Air Fryer recipes are healthy to eat and takes control over your weight gain issues

With Air Fryer, you can prepare breakfasts, salads, snacks, risotto, meat & seafood meals, vegetarian meals, appetizers, desserts and so much with a versatile Air Fryer.

In this unique Ninja Air Fryer cookbook, you will find an exclusive collection of 150 recipes to prepare diverse cuisines at the comfort of your home. Now you can cook hand-picked recipes from your favorite ingredients including breakfasts, snacks, sides, vegetarian meals, meat meals, appetizers, main course, and desserts

Get started to explore the exciting world of Air Fryer. Get ready to welcome a revolutionary way of preparing healthy fried recipes for your whole family.

Breakfast Recipes

Cheesy Ham Sandwich

(Ready in about: 10 minutes | **Serves:** 1)

Ingredients:

- 2 slices of American cheese
- 1 slice of ham
- 2 slices of bread
- 2 tsp butter

Instructions:

1. Preheat the Ninja Air fryer to 370°F. Spread 1 teaspoon of butter on the outside of each of the bread slices.
2. Place one cheese slice on the inside of one bread slice, top with ham slice and another cheese slice. Cover with the second bread slice to create the sandwich.
3. Place into the air fryer basket and cook for 4 minutes on Air Fry mode. Flip the sandwich and cook for an additional 4 minutes.
4. When the timer beeps, remove the sandwich, cut diagonally and serve immediately with ketchup or chutney.

Sausage Omelet

(Ready in about: 16 minutes | **Serves:** 2)

Ingredients:

- 1 sausage link; sliced
- 2 eggs; whisked
- 1 tbsp. olive oil
- 1 tbsp. cheddar cheese; grated
- 1 tbsp. cilantro; chopped.
- 4 cherry tomatoes; halved
- Salt and black pepper to taste

Instructions:

1. Put the tomatoes and sausage in the air fryer's basket and cook on air fryer mode at 360°F for 5 minutes
2. Take a pan that fits your air fryer, grease it with the oil and then transfer the tomatoes and sausage to the pan
3. In a bowl, mix all remaining ingredients and stir. Pour this over the sausage and tomato mixture, spread and place the pan in the air fryer; cook at 360°F for 6 minutes more. Serve immediately and enjoy.

Herbed Omelet

(Ready in about: 20 minutes | **Serves:** 4)

Ingredients:

- 6 eggs; whisked
- 2 tbsp. parmesan cheese; grated
- 1 tbsp. tarragon; chopped.
- 2 tbsp. chives; chopped.
- 4 tbsp. heavy cream
- 1 tbsp. parsley; chopped.
- Salt and black pepper to taste

Instructions:

1. In a bowl, mix all ingredients except for the parmesan and whisk well. Pour this into a pan that fits your air fryer, place it in preheated fryer and cook on air fryer mode at 350°F for 15 minutes
2. Divide the omelet between plates and serve with the parmesan sprinkled on top

Raspberry Pancake

(Ready in about: 15 minutes | **Serves:** 4)

Ingredients:

- ½ cup frozen raspberries, thawed
- 1 cup brown sugar
- 2 cups all-purpose flour
- 1 cup milk
- 3 eggs, beaten
- 2 tbsp maple syrup
- 1 tsp baking powder
- 1 ½ tsp vanilla extract
- Cooking spray
- Pinch of salt

Instructions:

1. Preheat the Ninja Air fryer to 390 F. In a bowl, mix the sifted flour, baking powder, salt, milk, eggs, vanilla extract, sugar, and maple syrup, until smooth. Gently stir in the raspberries.
2. Grease the basket of your Air fryer with cooking spray. Drop the batter into the basket. Cook for 10 minutes on Air Fry mode. Serve the pancake right away.

Mozzarella and Egg in a Cup

(Ready in about: 20 minutes | **Serves:** 2)

Ingredients:

- 2 slices bread
- 2 eggs
- 4 tomato slices
- 2 prosciutto slices, chopped
- 2 tbsp grated mozzarella
- 2 tbsp mayonnaise
- Cooking spray
- Salt and pepper, to taste

Instructions:

1. Preheat the Ninja Air fryer to 320°F. Grease two large ramekins with cooking spray. Place one bread slice in the bottom of each ramekin.
2. Arrange 1 prosciutto slice and 2 tomato slices on top of each bread slice.
3. Divide the mozzarella between the ramekins. Crack the eggs over the mozzarella.
4. Season with salt and pepper. Cook for 10 minutes on Air Fry mode. Top with mayonnaise.

Tuna Sandwiches

(Ready in about: 15 Minutes | **Serves:** 4)

Ingredients:

- 16 oz. canned tuna; drained
- 2 green onions; chopped
- 3 English muffins; halved
- 3 tbsp butter
- ¼ cup mayonnaise
- 2 tbsp mustard
- 1 tbsp lemon juice
- 6 provolone cheese

Instructions:

1. In a bowl; mix tuna with mayo, lemon juice, mustard and green onions and stir
2. Grease muffin halves with the butter, place them in preheated air fryer and bake them at 350°F, for 4 minutes. Spread tuna mix on muffin halves; top each with provolone cheese, return sandwiches to air fryer and cook them for 4 minutes; divide among plates and serve for breakfast right away

Cheesy Ham Eggplant Boats

(Ready in about: 17 minutes | **Serves:** 2)

Ingredients:

- 1 cup mozzarella cheese, shredded
- 2 eggplants
- 1 tsp dried parsley
- 6 ham slices, chopped
- Salt and pepper, to taste
- Cooking spray

Instructions:

1. Preheat the Ninja Air fryer to 330 F. Grease the air fryer basket with cooking spray; set aside. Cut the eggplants lengthwise in half and scoop some of the flesh out, leaving the skin intact. Season with salt and pepper.
2. Chop the scooped flesh and mix with mozzarella cheese, salt, and pepper.
3. Divide the cheese mixture between the eggplant halves. Cover with ham slices, and sprinkle with parsley.
4. Put the eggplant in the greased basket and cook for 12 minutes on Air Fry mode. Serve with a fresh salad.

Breakfast Sausage Rolls

(Ready in about: 16 minutes | **Serves:** 4)

Ingredients:

- 8 crescent roll dough pieces; separated
- 8 small sausages
- 8 cheddar cheese slices

Instructions:

1. Unroll the crescent roll pieces on a working surface and place one sausage and one slice of cheese on each.
2. Wrap the sausage and cheese with each roll and seal the edges
3. Place 4 wraps in your air fryer, cook at 380°F for 3 minutes on air fryer mode and transfer to a plate. Repeat with the remaining 4 sausage rolls and serve.

Italian Sausage Patties

(Ready in about: 20 minutes | **Serves:** 4)

Ingredients:
- 1 lb. ground Italian sausage
- ¼ cup breadcrumbs
- 1 tsp dried parsley
- 1 tsp red pepper Flakes
- 1 egg, beaten
- ¼ tsp garlic powder
- ½ tsp salt
- ¼ tsp black pepper

Instructions:
1. Preheat the Air fryer to 350 F. Line the basket with parchment paper; set aside. Combine all ingredients in a large bowl. Use your hands (clean!) to combine the mixture thoroughly.
2. Make patties out of the sausage mixture and arrange them on the basket. Cook for 14 minutes on Air Fry mode.
3. After 7 minutes, flip each patty. Once ready, remove and serve with tzatziki sauce.

Cheesy Meat Omelet

(Ready in about: 20 minutes | **Serves:** 2)

Ingredients:
- 3 oz salami, chopped
- 1 beef sausage, chopped
- 4 slices prosciutto, chopped
- 1 cup grated mozzarella cheese
- 4 eggs
- 1 tbsp ketchup
- 1 tbsp chopped onion

Instructions:
1. Preheat the Ninja Air fryer to 350°F on Air Fry mode. Whisk the eggs with the ketchup, in a bowl. Stir in the onion.
2. Spritz the inside of the air fryer basket with a cooking spray. Add and brown the sausage for about 2 minutes.
3. Meanwhile, combine the egg mixture, mozzarella cheese, salami and prosciutto.
4. Pour the egg mixture over the sausage and stir it. Cook for about 10 minutes. Once the timer beeps, ensure the omelet is just set. Serve immediately.

Delicious Pizza

(Ready in about: 15 minutes | **Serves:** 2)

Ingredients:
- 8 mozzarella slices
- 2 tortillas
- 8 ham slices
- 2 tbsp tomato sauce
- 8 thin pineapple slices
- Fresh basil leaves, chopped

Instructions:
1. Preheat the Ninja Air fryer to 330°F. Spread each tortilla with tomato sauce. Scatter over the ham, pineapple, and mozzarella.
2. Place the pizza into your air fryer basket and cook for 10 minutes on Air Fry mode.
3. When the timer beeps, remove and allow to sit for 2 minutes before slicing. Sprinkle the basil over and serve with napkins.

Herbed Tomatoes Breakfast

(Ready in about: 25 minutes | **Serves:** 2)

Ingredients:

- 1 lb. cherry tomatoes; halved
- A drizzle of olive oil
- 1 tsp. basil; chopped
- 1 tsp. oregano; chopped
- 1 tsp. rosemary; chopped.
- 1 cucumber; chopped.
- 1 spring onion; chopped
- 1 tsp. cilantro; chopped
- Salt and black pepper to taste

Instructions:

1. Grease the tomatoes with the oil, season with salt and pepper and place them in your air fryer's basket.
2. Cook the tomatoes at 320°F for 20 minutes on air fryer mode and then transfer them to a bowl. Add all remaining ingredients, toss and serve

Cheesy Onion Omelet

(Ready in about: 10 minutes | **Serves:** 1)

Ingredients:

- 2 eggs
- ½ onion, sliced
- 1 tbsp olive oil
- 2 tbsp grated cheddar cheese
- 1 tsp soy sauce
- ¼ tsp pepper

Instructions:

1. Whisk the eggs along with the pepper, onion, and soy sauce, in a bowl, until well-combined.
2. Preheat the Ninja Air fryer to 350°F on Air Fry mode. Grease a baking tray with olive oil and pour in the egg mixture. Cook for 5-6 minutes.
3. Once the timer beeps, check to ensure the eggs have set. Top with the grated cheddar cheese. Fold the omelet in half and serve with a green salad.

Mediterranean Quiche

(Ready in about: 40 minutes | **Serves:** 2)

Ingredients:

- 4 eggs
- ¼ cup chopped kalamata olives
- ¼ cup chopped onion
- ½ cup milk
- ½ cup chopped tomatoes
- 1 cup crumbled feta cheese
- 1 tbsp chopped basil
- 1 tbsp chopped oregano
- 2 tbsp olive oil
- Salt and pepper to taste

Instructions:

1. Preheat the Ninja Air fryer to 340°F. Brush a pie pan with the olive oil. Beat the eggs along with the milk, salt, and pepper. Stir in all of the remaining ingredients.
2. Pour the egg mixture into the pan. Cook for 30 minutes on Air Fry mode. Leave to cool before serving.

Delicious Doughnuts

(Ready in about: 28 Minutes | **Serves:** 6)

Ingredients:

- ½ cup sugar
- 2 ¼ cups white flour
- ⅓ cup caster sugar
- 4 tbsp butter; soft
- 1 ½ tsp baking powder
- 1 tsp cinnamon powder
- 2 egg yolks
- ½ cup sour cream

Instructions:

1. In a bowl; mix 2 tablespoon butter with simple sugar and egg yolks and whisk well
2. Add half of the sour cream and stir.
3. In another bowls; mix flour with baking powder, stir and also add to eggs mix
4. Stir well until you obtain a dough, transfer it to a floured working surface; roll it out and cut big circles with smaller ones in the middle.
5. Brush doughnuts with the rest of the butter; heat up your air fryer at 360°F; place doughnuts inside and cook them for 8 minutes on air fryer mode
6. In a bowl; mix cinnamon with caster sugar and stir. Arrange doughnuts on plates and dip them in cinnamon and sugar before serving.

Egg Rolls

(Ready in about: 18 minutes | **Serves:** 3)

Ingredients:

- 1 package egg roll wrappers (12 wrappers)
- 1 large grated carrot
- 2 garlic cloves, minced
- ½ onion, chopped
- 1 cup grated mozzarella cheese
- 1 cup ground beef
- 2 tsp olive oil
- ¼ tsp salt
- ¼ tsp pepper

Instructions:

1. Place the onion, garlic, carrot, and beef in a saucepan over medium heat, and cook for 6-7 minutes. Take the pan off the heat. Leave to cool for a few minutes, then mix in the mozzarella. Season to taste with salt, and pepper.
2. Preheat the Ninja Air fryer to 370 F. Grease the air fryer cooking basket with 1 tsp of the olive oil and set aside.
3. Lay the egg roll sheets onto a dry and clean surface; divide the mixture between them.
4. Roll the egg rolls and tuck the corners and edges in to create secure rolls.
5. Lower the rolls into the air fryer cooking basket and brush them with the remaining olive oil. Cook for 13 minutes on Air Fry mode.
6. Once ready, check if the rolls are golden and crispy. Serve with green salad.

Breakfast Potatoes

(Ready in about: 25 minutes | **Serves:** 4)

Ingredients:
- 1½ lbs. gold potatoes; cubed
- 1 tbsp. sweet paprika
- 1 tbsp. cilantro; chopped.
- 4 oz. Greek yogurt
- 2 tbsp. olive oil
- Salt and black pepper to taste

Instructions:
1. Put the potatoes in your air fryer and then add the oil, salt, pepper and paprika.
2. Stir and cook on air fryer mode at 360°F for 20 minutes. Transfer the potatoes to a bowl and add the yogurt and cilantro. Toss, serve and enjoy

Paprika Shirred Eggs

(Ready in about: 20 minutes | **Serves:** 2)

Ingredients:
- 4 slices of ham
- 4 eggs, divided
- 3 tbsp Parmesan cheese
- 2 tbsp heavy cream
- 2 tsp chopped chives
- 2 tsp butter, for greasing
- ¼ tsp paprika
- ¼ tsp pepper

Instructions:
1. Preheat the Ninja Air fryer to 320°F. Grease a pie pan with the butter. Arrange the ham slices on the bottom of the pan to cover it completely. Use more slices if needed.
2. Whisk one egg along with the heavy cream, salt, and pepper, in a small bowl.
3. Pour the mixture over the ham slices. Crack the other eggs over the ham.
4. Scatter Parmesan cheese over and cook for 14 minutes on Air Fry mode. Sprinkle with paprika and garnish with chives.

Chicken on Green Bed

(Ready in about: 20 minutes | **Serves:** 1)

Ingredients:
- 3 large kale leaves, chopped
- 1 garlic clove, minced
- 3 tbsp olive oil, divided
- 1 tsp balsamic vinegar
- 4 oz chicken breasts, cubed
- ½ cup baby spinach leaves
- ½ cup shredded romaine lettuce
- Salt and pepper, to taste

Instructions:
1. Preheat the Ninja Air fryer to 390°F. Place the chicken in a bowl along with 1 tbsp olive oil and garlic. Season with salt and pepper; toss to combine.
2. Place on a lined baking dish and cook for 14 minutes on Roast mode in your Ninja Air fryer.
3. Meanwhile, add the greens in a large bowl. Pour the remaining olive oil, balsamic vinegar, salt, and pepper, and toss to combine.
4. When the timer rings out, remove the chicken from the Air Fryer. Arrange the greens on a serving platter and top with the chicken, to serve.

Chicken and Spinach Casserole

(Ready in about: 30 minutes | **Serves:** 4)

Ingredients:
- 1 lb. chicken meat; ground
- 1 tbsp. olive oil
- ½ tsp. sweet paprika
- 12 eggs; whisked
- 1 cup baby spinach
- Salt and black pepper to taste

Instructions:
1. In a bowl, whisk the eggs with the salt, pepper and paprika. Then add the spinach and chicken and mix well.
2. Heat up your air fryer at 350°F; add the oil and allow it to heat up
3. Add the chicken and spinach mix, cover and cook for 25 minutes on air fryer mode. Divide between plates and serve hot

Bread Pudding

(Ready in about: 45 minutes | **Serves:** 3)

Ingredients:
- 8 slices of bread
- 2 eggs
- ¼ cup sugar
- ½ cup buttermilk
- ¼ cup honey
- 1 cup milk
- ½ tsp vanilla extract
- 4 tbsp raisins
- 2 tbsp chopped hazelnuts
- 2 tbsp butter, softened
- Cinnamon for garnish

Instructions:
1. Preheat the Ninja Air fryer to 310°F. Beat the eggs along with the buttermilk, honey, milk, vanilla, sugar, and butter.
2. Stir in raisins and hazelnuts. Cut the bread into cubes and place it in a bowl. Pour the milk mixture over the bread. Let soak for about 10 minutes.
3. Cook the bread pudding for 25 minutes on Roast mode. Leave the dessert to cool for 5 minutes, then invert onto a plate and sprinkle with cinnamon to serve.

Roasted Peppers Frittata

(Ready in about: 30 minutes | **Serves:** 6)

Ingredients:

- 6 oz. jarred roasted red bell peppers; chopped.
- ½ cup parmesan cheese; grated
- 2 tbsp. parsley; chopped.
- 2 tbsp. chives; chopped.
- 6 tbsp. ricotta cheese
- 12 eggs; whisked
- 3 garlic cloves; minced
- A drizzle of olive oil
- Salt and black pepper to taste

Instructions:

1. In a bowl, mix the bell peppers with the eggs, garlic, parsley, salt, pepper, chives and ricotta; whisk well.
2. Heat up your air fryer at 300°F, add the oil and spread. Add the egg mixture, spread, sprinkle the parmesan on top and cook on air fryer mode for 20 minutes. Divide between plates and serve.

Cheesy Crispy Straws

(Ready in about: 45 minutes | **Serves:** 8)

Ingredients:

- 3 ½ oz oats
- 5 oz cheddar cheese
- 1 red onion, diced
- 2 cups cauliflower florets, steamed
- 1 egg
- 1 tsp mustard
- Salt and pepper, to taste

Instructions:

1. Preheat the Ninja Air fryer to 350°F. Add the oats in a food processor and process until they resemble breadcrumbs.
2. Place the steamed florets in a cheesecloth and squeeze out the excess liquid.
3. Put the florets in a large bowl, and add the rest of the ingredients to the bowl.
4. Mix well with your hands, to combine the ingredients thoroughly.
5. Take a little bit of the mixture and twist it into a straw. Place in the lined air fryer basket; repeat with the rest of the mixture. Cook for 10 minutes on Air Fry mode.
6. After 5 minutes, turn them over and cook for an additional 10 minutes.

Poultry Recipes

Delicious Wings

(**Ready in about:** 4 hours 20 minutes | **Serves:** 2)

Ingredients:

- 8 chicken wings
- 2 tbsp cornstarch
- 2 tbsp tom yum paste
- 1 tbsp water
- 2 tbsp potato starch
- ½ tsp baking powder

Instructions:

1. Combine the tom yum paste and water, in a small bowl. Place the wings in a large bowl, add the tom yum mixture and coat well.
2. Cover the bowl and refrigerate for 4 hours. Preheat the Ninja Air fryer to 370°F. Combine the baking powder, cornstarch, and potato starch. Dip each wing in the starch mixture.
3. Place on a lined baking dish in the Air fryer and cook for 7 minutes on Air Fry mode. Flip over and cook for 5 to 7 minutes more.

Chicken Kabobs

(**Ready in about:** 20 minutes | **Serves:** 4)

Ingredients:

- 4 chicken breasts, skinless and cubed
- Juice from 1 Lime
- ½ tsp ground paprika
- 4 tbsp honey
- Salt and pepper to taste

Instructions:

1. Preheat your Ninja Air Fryer to 360°F. In a large bowl, combine the honey, soy sauce, lime juice, paprika, salt, and pepper. Add in the chicken cubes and toss to coat.
2. Load 8 small skewers with honey-glazed chicken. Lay the kabobs into the air fryer basket and cook for 15 minutes. After 8 minutes, turn the kabobs over.
3. Drizzle the remaining honey sauce and serve with sautéed veggies.

Fried Whole Chicken

(**Ready in about:** 30 minutes | **Serves:** 8)

Ingredients:

- 1 whole chicken; cut into medium pieces
- 3 tbsp. white wine
- 1 tbsp. ginger; grated
- 1 cup chicken stock
- 2 carrots; chopped.
- Salt and black pepper to taste

Instructions:

1. In a pan that fits your air fryer, mix all of the ingredients
2. Put the pan in the air fryer and cook on air fryer mode 370°F for 20 minutes. Divide between plates and serve.

Basil and Cheese Chicken

(Ready in about: 25 minutes | **Serves:** 4)

Ingredients:

- 2 large chicken breasts, skinless
- 4 cherry tomatoes, halved
- 4 slices cheddar cheese
- A handful of fresh basil leaves
- 2 tbsp olive oil
- Salt and pepper to taste

Instructions:

1. Preheat your Ninja Air fryer to 370°F. With a sharp knife, cut a slit into the side of each chicken breast.
2. Put 2 slices of cheese, 3 to 4 basil leaves, and 4 cherry tomato halves into each slit. Use toothpicks to keep the chicken breasts closed. Season the meat with salt and pepper, and brush with some olive oil.
3. Grease the air fryer basket with the remaining olive oil and place the chicken breasts in the basket; cook for 12 minutes. After 6 minutes, turn the breasts over.
4. Once ready, leave to sit the chicken breasts, then slice each one in half and serve with salad.

Chicken Burgers with Avocado

(Ready in about: 15 minutes | **Serves:** 8)

Ingredients:

- 1 lb. ground chicken
- 1 Avocado, sliced
- ½ cup mayonnaise
- 1 tomato, sliced
- 1 red onion, chopped
- 1 egg, beaten
- 4 buns, halved
- 1 small red potato, shredded
- A pinch of ground cumin
- A pinch of ground chili
- Fresh cilantro, chopped
- Salt and pepper to taste
- Cooking spray

Instructions:

1. Preheat your Ninja Air fryer to 360°F. Mix the chicken, onion, egg, potato, cumin, chili, cilantro, salt, and pepper in a large bowl with your hands until you have an even burger mixture.
2. Shape the mixture into 8 patties. Grease your air fryer basket with cooking spray. Arrange the burgers onto the basket. Cook for 10 minutes. After 5 minutes, shake the patties.
3. To assemble your burgers, spread mayonnaise on the bottom of each half of the buns, top with a chicken patty, then put over a tomato slice.
4. Cover with the other half of the buns and arrange on a serving platter to serve.

Korean Barbecued Satay

(**Ready in about:** 4h 15 minutes | **Serves:** 4)

Ingredients:

- 1 lb. boneless, skinless chicken tenders
- 4 cloves garlic, chopped
- 4 scallions, chopped
- ½ cup pineapple juice
- ½ cup soy sauce
- ⅓ cup sesame oil
- 2 tsp sesame seeds, toasted
- 1 tsp fresh ginger, grated
- 1 pinch black pepper

Instructions:

1. Skew each tender and trim any excess fat. Mix the other ingredients in one large bowl. Add the skewered chicken and place in the fridge for 4 to 24 hours.
2. Preheat the Ninja Air fryer to 375°F. Using a paper towel, pat the chicken dry. Fry for 10 minutes on Air Fry mode.

Buttered Turkey

(**Ready in about:** 25 minutes | **Serves:** 6)

Ingredients:

- 6 turkey breasts, boneless and skinless
- 2 cups panko breadcrumbs
- 1 stick butter, melted
- ½ tsp cayenne pepper
- ½ tsp black pepper
- 1 tsp salt

Instructions:

1. In a bowl, combine the panko breadcrumbs, half of the black pepper, the cayenne pepper, and half of the salt. In another bowl, combine the melted butter with salt and pepper.
2. Brush the butter mixture over the turkey breast. Coat the turkey with the panko mixture. Arrange on a lined air fryer basket.
3. Cook for 15 minutes at 390°F on Air Fry mode, flipping the meat after 8 minutes.

Easy Chicken Thighs

(**Ready in about:** 21 minutes | **Serves:** 6)

Ingredients:

- 8 chicken thighs
- 1 tbsp. ginger; grated
- 1 tbsp. sweet paprika
- 1 tbsp. lime juice
- 2 tbsp. olive oil
- 1 tbsp. turmeric powder
- 1 tbsp. coriander; ground
- Salt and black pepper to taste

Instructions:

1. Place all the ingredients in a bowl and toss well
2. Transfer the chicken thighs to your air fryer's basket and cook on air fryer mode at 370°F for 8 minutes on each side
3. Divide between plates and serve with a side salad.

Awesome Oregano Chicken Thighs

(Ready in about: 35 minutes | **Serves:** 4)

Ingredients:
- 8 chicken thighs
- 4 tsp. oregano; chopped.
- ½ tsp. sweet paprika
- 2 garlic cloves; minced
- 1 red onion; chopped.
- 2 tbsp. olive oil
- Salt and black pepper to taste

Instructions:
1. In a baking dish that fits your air fryer, place all of the ingredients and mix well.
2. Transfer the dish to your air fryer and cook on air fryer mode at 400°F for 30 minutes, shaking halfway. Divide between plates and serve

Herbed Chicken

(Ready in about: 35 minutes | **Serves:** 8)

Ingredients:
- 8 chicken thighs
- 3 garlic cloves; minced
- 1 cup chicken stock
- ½ tsp. basil; dried
- ½ tsp. thyme; dried
- ½ tsp. oregano; dried
- ¼ cup cheddar cheese; grated
- ¼ cup heavy cream
- 3 tbsp. butter; melted
- 1 tbsp. mustard
- Salt and black pepper to taste

Instructions:
1. In a baking dish that fits your air fryer, place all ingredients except the cheddar cheese; mix well
2. Transfer the dish to your air fryer and cook on air fryer mode at 370°F for 25 minutes
3. Sprinkle the cheese on top and cook for 5 more minutes. Divide everything between plates and serve.

Greek Chicken

(Ready in about: 45 minutes | **Serves:** 6)

Ingredients:
- 1 whole chicken (3 lb.), cut in pieces
- 3 garlic cloves, minced
- ½ cup white wine
- ½ cup olive oil
- Juice from 1 lemon
- 1 tbsp fresh thyme
- 1 tbsp fresh rosemary
- 1 tbsp chopped fresh oregano
- Salt and black pepper, to taste

Instructions:
1. Preheat the Ninja Air fryer to 380° F. In a large bowl, combine the garlic, rosemary, thyme, olive oil, lemon juice, oregano, salt, and pepper.
2. Mix all ingredients very well and spread the mixture into the air fryer basket. Stir in the chicken. Sprinkle with wine and cook for 45 minutes on Air Fry mode.

Sweet Chicken Wings

(Ready in about: 20 minutes | **Serves:** 4)

Ingredients:
- 16 chicken wings
- 4 garlic cloves, minced
- ¾ cup potato starch
- ¼ cup butter
- ¼ cup honey
- ½ tsp salt

Instructions:
1. Preheat the Ninja Air fryer to 370°F. Rinse and pat dry the wings, and place them in a bowl. Add the starch to the bowl, and mix to coat the chicken.
2. Place the chicken in a baking dish that has been previously coated lightly with cooking oil. Cook for 5 minutes on Air Fry mode.
3. Meanwhile, whisk the rest of the ingredients together in a bowl. Pour the sauce over the wings and cook for another 10 minutes.

Lemon Chicken

(Ready in about: 60 minutes | **Serves:** 2)

Ingredients:
- 2 chicken breasts
- 2 rosemary sprigs
- ½ lemon, cut into wedges
- 1 tbsp oyster sauce
- 1 tbsp soy sauce
- ½ tbsp olive oil
- 3 tbsp brown sugar
- 1 tsp minced ginger

Instructions:
1. Place the ginger, soy sauce, and olive oil, in a bowl. Add the chicken and coat well. Cover the bowl and refrigerate for 30 minutes.
2. Preheat the air fryer to 370 F. Transfer the marinated chicken to the air fryer basket. Cook for about 6 minutes on Air Fry mode.
3. Mix the oyster sauce, rosemary and brown sugar in a small bowl. Pour the sauce over the chicken. Arrange the lemon wedges in the dish. Return to the air fryer and cook for 13 more minutes on Air Fry mode.

Asian Chicken

(Ready in about: 35 minutes | **Serves:** 4)

Ingredients:
- 1 lb. chicken, cut in stripes
- 3 green peppers, cut in stripes
- 1 large onion
- 2 tomatoes, cubed
- 1 pinch ginger
- 1 pinch fresh and chopped coriander
- 1 tbsp mustard
- 2 tbsp oil
- 1 tbsp cumin powder
- Salt and black pepper

Instructions:
1. Heat the oil in a deep pan. Add in the mustard, onion, ginger, cumin and green chili peppers. Sauté the mixture for 2-3 minutes.
2. Then, add the tomatoes, coriander, and salt and keep stirring. Preheat the Ninja Air fryer to 380° F.
3. Coat the chicken with oil, salt, and pepper and cook for 25 minutes on Air Fry mode. Remove from the Air Fryer and pour the sauce over and around.

Chicken Tenders with Rice

(**Ready in about:** 60 minutes | **Serves:** 3)

Ingredients:
- 1 lb. chicken tenderloins
- 1 can condensed cream chicken soup
- 1 package instant long grain rice
- 2 cups water
- 1 cup chopped broccoli
- 1 tbsp minced garlic

Instructions:
1. Preheat the Air Fryer to 390° F, and place the chicken quarters in the Air Fryer. Season with salt, pepper and a tbsp of oil and cook for 30 minutes on Roast mode.
2. Meanwhile, in a large bowl, mix rice, water, minced garlic, soup, and broccoli. Combine the mixture very well.
3. Remove the chicken from the Air fryer and place it on a platter to drain. Spread the rice mixture on the bottom of the dish and place the chicken on top of the rice. Cook again for 30 minutes on Roast mode.

Fried Chicken Wings

(**Ready in about:** 55 minutes | **Serves:** 4)

Ingredients:
- 16 chicken wings
- 4 tbsp. garlic; minced
- ¼ cup butter; melted
- ¼ cup clover honey
- Salt and black pepper to taste

Instructions:
1. Put the chicken wings in your air fryer's basket and season with salt and pepper.
2. Cook on air fryer mode at 380°F for 25 minutes, then at 400°F for 5 minutes and put it in a bowl
3. Melt the butter in a pan over medium-high heat; then add the garlic, stir and sauté for 5 minutes
4. Add salt, pepper, the air fried chicken and the honey; stir and simmer for 10 minutes more over medium heat. Divide the chicken wings and the sauce between plates and serve.

Bleu Chicken

(Ready in about: 40 minutes | **Serves:** 4)

Ingredients:

- 4 skinless and boneless chicken breasts
- 4 slices Swiss cheese
- 4 slices ham
- 1 cup heavy whipping cream
- ½ cup dry white wine
- 4 tbsp butter
- 3 tbsp all-purpose flour
- 1 tsp paprika
- 1 tsp chicken bouillon granules

Instructions:

1. Preheat the Ninja Air fryer to 380° F. Pound the chicken breasts and put a slice of ham and then a slice of Swiss cheese on each of the breasts. Fold the edges over the filling and secure the sides with toothpicks.
2. In a medium bowl, combine the paprika and the flour and coat the chicken pieces.
3. Fry the chicken for 20 minutes on Air Fry mode. Meanwhile, in a large skillet over medium heat, melt the butter and add the bouillon and the wine. Reduce the heat to low.
4. Add in the heavy cream and let simmer for 20-25 minutes. When the chicken is done, remove to a serving platter and drizzle with the sauce. Serve hot.

Turkey Nuggets

(Ready in about: 20 minutes | **Serves:** 2)

Ingredients:

- 8 oz turkey breast, boneless and skinless
- 1 cup breadcrumbs
- 1 egg, beaten
- 1 tbsp dried thyme
- ½ tsp dried parsley
- Salt and pepper, to taste

Instructions:

1. Preheat the Ninja Air fryer to 350°F. Mince the turkey in a food processor. Transfer to a bowl. Stir in the thyme and parsley, and season with salt and pepper.
2. Take a nugget-sized piece of the turkey mixture and shape it into a ball, or another form.
3. Dip it in the breadcrumbs, then egg, then in the breadcrumbs again. Place the nuggets onto a prepared baking dish. Cook for 10 minutes on Air Fry mode.

Salsa Verde Chicken Breast.

(Ready in about: 30 minutes | **Serves:** 4)

Ingredients:

- 16 oz. salsa Verde
- ¼ cup parsley; chopped.
- 1 tsp. sweet paprika
- 1 tbsp. avocado oil
- 1 lb. chicken breast; boneless and skinless
- 1½ cups cheddar cheese; grated
- Salt and black pepper to taste

Instructions:

1. In a baking dish that fits your air fryer, place all ingredients except the cheese; toss well
2. Put the pan into the fryer and cook on air fryer mode at 380°F for 17 minutes
3. Sprinkle with the cheese and cook for 3-4 minutes more. Divide between plates and serve.

Chicken Breasts and Veggies.

(Ready in about: 30 minutes | **Serves:** 4)

Ingredients:

- 2 lbs. chicken breasts; skinless and boneless
- 12 brown mushrooms; halved
- 1 red onion; chopped.
- 2 garlic cloves; minced
- 2 tbsp. olive oil
- 2 tbsp. cheddar cheese; shredded
- 1 red bell pepper; chopped.
- 1 green bell pepper; roughly chopped.
- Salt and black pepper to taste

Instructions:

1. Season the chicken breasts with salt and pepper and then rub with the garlic and 1 tbsp. of the oil
2. Place the chicken breasts in your preheated air fryer's basket, cook on air fryer mode at 390°F for 6 minutes on each side and divide between plates.
3. Heat up a pan with the remaining 1 tbsp. of the oil over medium heat; add the onions, stir and cook for 2 minutes
4. Add the mushrooms and bell peppers, stir and cook for 5-6 minutes more
5. Divide this next to the chicken, sprinkle the cheese all over and serve.

Drumsticks

(Ready in about: 50 minutes | **Serves:** 4)

Ingredients:

- 1 lb. drumsticks
- 2 tsp dijon mustard.
- 2 tbsp honey
- Salt and pepper to taste
- Cooking spray

Instructions:

1. Combine the honey, mustard, salt, and pepper in a large bowl. Add in the chicken and toss to coat. Cover and put in the fridge for 30 minutes.
2. Preheat your Ninja Air fryer to 380°F. Grease the air fryer basket with cooking spray. Arrange the drumsticks on the basket. Cook for 20 minutes on Air Fry mode. After 10 minutes, shake the drumsticks.

Tomato Chicken

(Ready in about: 30 minutes | **Serves:** 6)

Ingredients:

- 14 oz. tomato sauce
- 6 oz. mozzarella cheese; grated
- 1 tbsp. olive oil
- 1 tsp. oregano; dried
- 1 tsp. garlic powder
- 4 medium chicken breasts; skinless and boneless
- Salt and black pepper to taste

Instructions:

1. Put the chicken in your air fryer and season with salt, pepper, garlic powder and the oregano.
2. Cook the chicken at 360°F for 5 minutes on air fryer mode; then transfer to a pan that fits your air fryer, greased with the oil
3. Add the tomato sauce, sprinkle the mozzarella on top, place the pan in the fryer and cook on air fryer mode at 350°F for 15 minutes more. Divide between plates and serve

Soy Sauce Chicken

(Ready in about: 50 minutes | **Serves:** 6)

Ingredients:

- 1 whole chicken; cut into pieces
- 1 tsp. sesame oil
- 2 tsp. soy sauce
- 1 chili pepper; minced
- 1 tbsp. ginger; grated
- Salt and black pepper to taste

Instructions:

1. In a bowl, mix the chicken with all the other ingredients and rub well
2. Transfer the chicken pieces to your air fryer's basket
3. Cook on air fryer mode at 400°F for 30 minutes and then at 380°F for 10 minutes more. Divide everything between plates and serve

Chicken Thighs

(Ready in about: 4 hours 40 minutes | **Serves:** 6)

Ingredients:

- 1 ½ lb. chicken thighs
- 2 cups flour
- 2 cups buttermilk
- 2 tsp black pepper
- 1 tsp cayenne pepper
- 3 tsp salt divided
- 1 tbsp paprika
- 1 tbsp baking powder

Instructions:

1. Rinse and pat dry the chicken thighs. Place the chicken thighs in a bowl. Add cayenne pepper, 2 tsp salt, black pepper, and buttermilk, and stir to coat well.
2. Refrigerate for 4 hours. Preheat the Ninja Air fryer to 350°F. In another bowl, mix the flour, paprika, 1 tsp salt, and baking powder.
3. Dredge half of the chicken thighs, one at a time, in the flour, and then place on a lined dish. Cook for 18 minutes on Air Fry mode, flipping once halfway through. Repeat with the other batch.

Glazed Chicken and Apples

(Ready in about: 30 minutes | **Serves:** 4)

Ingredients:

- 6 chicken thighs; skin-on
- 1 tbsp. rosemary; chopped
- 2 tbsp. honey
- 1 tbsp. mustard
- 3 apples; cored and sliced
- ⅔ cup apple cider
- 2 tbsp. olive oil
- Salt and black pepper to taste

Instructions:

1. Heat up a pan that fits your air fryer with 1 tbsp. of the oil over medium heat.
2. Add the cider, honey and mustard; whisk
3. Bring to a simmer and take off the heat.
4. Add the chicken, apples, salt, pepper and rosemary; toss
5. Place the pan in your air fryer and cook on air fryer mode at 390°F for 17 minutes. Divide between plates and serve.

Meat Recipes

Coconut Pork

(Ready in about: 20 minutes | **Serves:** 4)

Ingredients:

- 7 oz. coconut milk
- 14 oz. pork chops; cut into strips
- 2 tsp. chili paste
- 2 tbsp. olive oil
- 3 tbsp. soy sauce
- 2 garlic cloves; minced
- 1 shallot; chopped.
- 1 tsp. ginger; grated
- Salt and black pepper to taste

Instructions:

1. In a baking dish that fits your air fryer, mix the pork with the ginger, chili paste, garlic, shallots, oil soy sauce, salt and pepper; toss well
2. Place the pan in the fryer and cook on air fryer mode at 400°F for 12 minutes, shaking the fryer halfway
3. Add the coconut milk, toss and cook for 3-4 minutes more. Divide everything into bowls and serve.

Thai Roasted Beef

(Ready in about: 4 hours 20 minutes | **Serves:** 2)

Ingredients:

- 1 lb. ground beef
- Thumb-sized piece of ginger, chopped
- 3 chilies, deseeded and chopped
- 4 garlic cloves, chopped
- Juice of 1 lime
- 2 tbsp oil
- 2 tbsp fish sauce
- 2 tbsp soy sauce
- 2 tbsp mirin
- 2 tbsp basil, chopped
- 2 tbsp coriander, chopped
- 1 tsp brown sugar
- ½ tsp salt
- ½ tsp pepper

Instructions:

1. Place all ingredients, except beef, salt, and pepper, in a blender; pulse until smooth.
2. Season the beef with salt and pepper. Place the meat and Thai mixture in a zipper bag. Shake well to combine and let marinate in the fridge for about 4 hours.
3. Preheat the Ninja Air fryer to 350°F. Place the beef in the air fryer basket and cook for about 12 minutes, or more if you like it well done, on Air Fry mode. Let sit for 5 minutes before serving.

Greek Style Lamb Chops

(Ready in about: 24 minutes | **Serves:** 4)

Ingredients:

- 4 lamb chops
- 1 cup green olives; pitted and sliced
- 3 garlic cloves; minced
- 2 tbsp. olive oil
- 1 tsp. marjoram; dried
- 1 tsp. thyme; dried
- ½ cup veggie stock
- 1 tbsp. white flour
- Salt and black pepper to taste

Instructions:

1. Place all ingredients except the olives in a bowl and mix well. Then put in the fridge for 10 minutes.
2. Transfer the lamb chops to your air fryer's basket and cook on air fryer mode at 390°F for 7 minutes on each side
3. Divide the lamb chops between plates, sprinkle the olives on top and serve

Beef Shapes

(Ready in about: 40 minutes | **Serves:** 12)

Ingredients:

- 1 ½ lb. ground beef
- 3 garlic cloves, minced
- ½ cup minced onion
- 2 tbsp chopped mint leaves
- 1 tbsp chopped parsley
- 2 tsp cumin
- ½ tsp ground ginger
- 2 tsp paprika
- 2 tsp coriander seeds
- ½ tsp cayenne pepper
- 1 tsp salt

Instructions:

1. Soak 24 skewers in water, until ready to use. Preheat the Ninja Air fryer to 330°F. Combine all ingredients in a large bowl.
2. Make sure to mix well with your hands until the herbs and spices are evenly distributed, and the mixture is well incorporated.
3. Shape the beef mixture into 12 shapes around 2 skewers. Cook for 12 - 15 minutes on Air Fry mode, or until preferred doneness. Serve with tzatziki sauce and enjoy.

Peppercorn Meatloaf Delight

(Ready in about: 35 minutes | **Serves:** 8)

Ingredients:

- 4 lb. ground beef
- 10 whole peppercorns, for garnishing
- 1 cup breadcrumbs
- 1 tbsp Worcestershire sauce
- 3 tbsp ketchup
- 1 tbsp oregano
- 1 tbsp parsley
- 1 tbsp basil
- 1 onion, diced
- ½ tsp salt
- 1 tsp ground peppercorns

Instructions:

1. Preheat the Ninja Air fryer to 350°F. Place the beef in a large bowl. Add all of the ingredients except the whole peppercorns and the breadcrumbs.
2. Mix with your hand until well combined. Stir in the breadcrumbs. Put the meatloaf on a lined baking dish.
3. Insert in the air fryer and cook for 25 minutes on Air Fry mode. Garnish the meatloaf with the whole peppercorns and let cool slightly before serving.

Crispiest Roast Pork

(**Ready in about:** 50 minutes | **Serves:** 4)

Ingredients:

- 4 pork tenderloins
- ¾ tsp garlic powder
- 1 tsp five spice seasoning
- ½ tsp white pepper
- 1 tsp salt
- Cooking spray

Instructions:

1. Place the pork, white pepper, garlic powder, five seasoning, and salt into a bowl and toss to coat. Leave to marinate at room temperature for 30 minutes. Preheat the Ninja air fryer to 360°F.
2. Place the pork into the air fryer basket, greased with cooking spray and cook for 20 minutes. After 10 minutes, turn the tenderloins. Serve hot.

Beef Kabobs Recipe

(**Ready in about:** 20 Minutes | **Serves:** 4)

Ingredients:

- 2 red bell peppers; chopped
- 2 lb. sirloin steak; cut into medium pieces
- 1 red onion; chopped
- 1 zucchini; sliced
- ½ tbsp cumin; ground
- ¼ cup olive oil
- ¼ cup salsa
- Juice form 1 lime
- 2 tbsp chili powder
- 2 tbsp hot sauce
- Salt and black pepper to the taste

Instructions:

1. In a bowl; mix salsa with lime juice, oil, hot sauce, chili powder, cumin, salt and black pepper and whisk well.
2. Divide meat bell peppers, zucchini and onion on skewers, brush kabobs with the salsa mix you made earlier, put them in your preheated air fryer and cook on air fryer mode for 10 minutes at 370°F, flipping kabobs halfway. Divide among plates and serve with a side salad

Philippine Pork Chops

(**Ready in about:** 2 hours 20 minutes | **Serves:** 6)

Ingredients:

- 2 lb. pork chops
- 5 garlic cloves, coarsely chopped
- 2 bay leaves
- 1 tbsp peppercorns
- 2 tbsp soy sauce
- 1 tbsp peanut oil
- 1 tsp salt

Instructions:

1. Combine the bay leaves, soy sauce, garlic, salt, peppercorns, and oil, in a bowl. Rub the mixture onto the meat. Wrap the pork with a plastic foil and refrigerate for 2 hours. Preheat the Ninja Air fryer to 350°F.
2. Place the pork in the air fryer and cook for 10 minutes on Air Fry mode. Increase the temperature to 370 F, flip the chops, and cook for another 10 minutes. Discard bay leaves before serving.

Marinated Beef

(**Ready in about:** 30 minutes | **Serves:** 4)

Ingredients:

- 3 lbs. chuck roast; cut into thin strips
- 5 garlic cloves; minced
- 3 red peppers; dried and crushed
- ½ cup soy sauce
- ½ cup black soy sauce
- 1 tbsp. olive oil
- 2 tbsp. fish sauce

Instructions:

1. In a bowl, combine the beef with all ingredients; toss well and place in the fridge for 10 minutes.
2. Transfer the beef to your air fryer's basket and cook on air fryer mode at 380°F for 20 minutes. Serve with a side salad

Pork and Shallots

(**Ready in about:** 45 minutes | **Serves:** 4)

Ingredients:

- 1½ lbs. pork stew meat; cubed
- 3 oz. white mushrooms; sliced
- 16 oz. shallots; chopped.
- 2 oz. white wine
- 2 tbsp. chives; chopped.
- 2 tbsp. olive oil
- 1 tbsp. cilantro; chopped.
- 2 oz. canned tomatoes; cubed
- 2 garlic cloves; minced
- ½ cup beef stock
- Salt and black pepper to taste

Instructions:

1. Heat up a pan that fits your air fryer with the oil over medium heat.
2. Add the meat, stir and brown for 2 minutes.
3. Next, add the shallots, garlic, chives, salt, pepper and mushrooms; toss and cook for 2 minutes more.
4. Then add the mushrooms, tomatoes, wine and stock; stir well

5. Simmer for about 1 minute and then transfer the pan to your air fryer; cook on air fryer mode at 380°F for 30 minutes.
6. Add the cilantro and toss. Divide everything into bowls and serve

French Style Lamb

(**Ready in about:** 30 minutes | **Serves:** 4)

Ingredients:

- 1½ lbs. lamb chops
- ½ lbs. mushrooms; sliced
- 1 small yellow onion; chopped.
- 1 tsp. olive oil
- 1 tsp. oregano; dried
- ½ tsp. mint; dried
- 6 garlic cloves; minced
- 4 tomatoes; chopped.
- 2 tbsp. tomato paste
- A handful of cilantro; chopped.
- Salt and black pepper to taste

Instructions:

1. Heat up a pan that fits your air fryer with the oil over medium heat.
2. Add the lamb chops, salt, pepper, oregano and mint; toss and brown for 2-3 minutes
3. Add the mushrooms, onions, garlic, tomatoes and tomato paste; toss and cook for 2 more minutes.
4. Place the pan in the fryer and cook on air fryer mode at 400°F for 12 minutes more
5. Add the cilantro and toss. Divide everything between plates and serve

Pork Meatloaf

(**Ready in about:** 25 minutes | **Serves:** 4)

Ingredients:

- 1 lb. ground pork meat
- 1 yellow onion; chopped.
- 3 tbsp. breadcrumbs
- 1 tbsp. thyme; chopped.
- 1 oz. chorizo; chopped.
- 1 egg; whisked
- Cooking spray
- Salt and black pepper to taste

Instructions:

1. Place all of the ingredients (except the cooking spray) in a bowl and stir / combine well.
2. Transfer the mixture to a loaf pan, greased with cooking spray, that fits your air fryer
3. Place the pan in the fryer and cook on air fryer mode at 390°F for 20 minutes. Slice and serve

Pork Chops

(Ready in about: 25 minutes | **Serves:** 3)

Ingredients:

Topping:

- 1 small onion, sliced
- 1 cup sliced apples
- 1 tbsp apple cider vinegar
- 2 tbsp olive oil
- 2 tsp rosemary
- 2 tsp thyme
- ¼ tsp brown sugar

Meat:

- 3 pork chops
- 1 tbsp olive oil
- 1 tbsp apple cider vinegar
- ¼ tsp smoked paprika
- Salt and pepper, to taste

Instructions:

1. Preheat the Ninja Air fryer to 350°F. Place all topping ingredients in a baking dish, and then in the air fryer.
2. Cook for 4 minutes on Air Fry mode. Meanwhile, place the pork chops in a bowl. Add olive oil, vinegar, paprika, and season with salt and pepper. Stir to coat them well. Remove the topping from the dish.
3. Add the pork chops in the dish and cook for 10 minutes on Air Fry mode. Place the topping on top, return to the air fryer and cook for 5 more minutes.

Crunchy Lamb Rack

(Ready in about: 30 minutes | **Serves:** 4)

Ingredients:

- 1 ½ lb. rack of lamb
- 3 oz chopped cashews
- 1 garlic clove, minced
- 1 egg, beaten
- 1 tbsp breadcrumbs
- 1 tbsp olive oil
- 1 tbsp chopped rosemary
- Salt and pepper, to taste

Instructions:

1. Preheat the Ninja Air fryer to 320°F. Combine the olive oil with the garlic and brush this mixture onto the lamb.
2. Meanwhile, combine the rosemary, cashews, and breadcrumbs, in a small bowl. Brush the egg over the lambs, and then coat it with the cashew mixture.
3. Place the lamb in the air fryer and cook for 25 minutes on Air Fry mode. Increase the temperature to 390°F, and cook for an additional 5 minutes. Cover with a foil and let sit for a couple of minutes before serving.

Pork and Bell Peppers

(Ready in about: 32 minutes | **Serves:** 2)

Ingredients:
- 7 oz. pork tenderloin; cut into strips
- 1 green bell pepper; cut into strips
- 1 sweet onion; chopped.
- 1 red bell pepper; cut into strips
- 1 tbsp. olive oil
- 1 yellow bell pepper; cut in strips
- Salt and black pepper to taste

Instructions:
1. Place all of the ingredients into a pan that fits your air fryer and toss well.
2. Put the pan in the fryer and cook on air fryer mode at 390°F for 22 minutes. Divide the mix between plates and serve

Mustard Pork Chops

(Ready in about: 25 minutes | **Serves:** 6)

Ingredients:
- 2 pork chops
- 2 garlic cloves; minced
- 1 tsp. sweet paprika
- 1 tbsp. mustard
- ¼ cup olive oil
- Salt and black pepper to taste

Instructions:
1. Place all of the ingredients in a bowl and coat the pork chops well
2. Transfer the pork chops to your air fryer's basket and cook on air fryer mode at 400°F for 15 minutes. Divide the chops between plates and serve

BBQ Pork Ribs

(Ready in about: 4 h 35 minutes | **Serves:** 2)

Ingredients:
- 1 lb. pork ribs
- 3 garlic cloves, chopped
- 1 tbsp honey, plus more for brushing
- 4 tbsp barbecue sauce
- 1 tsp black pepper
- 1 tsp sesame oil
- 1 tsp soy sauce
- ½ tsp five spice powder
- 1 tsp salt

Instructions:
1. Chop the ribs into smaller pieces and place in a large bowl. In a separate bowl, whisk together all of the other ingredients.
2. Add to the bowl with the pork, and mix until the pork is thoroughly coated.
3. Cover the bowl, place it in the fridge, and let it marinade for about 4 hours. Preheat the Ninja Air fryer to 350°F.
4. Place the ribs in the basket of the air fryer. Cook for 15 minutes on Air Fry mode. After, brush the ribs with some honey and cook for 15 more minutes.

Pork Ribs

(Ready in about: 4 hours 55 minutes | **Serves:** 6)

Ingredients:

- 2 lb. pork ribs
- 4 garlic cloves, minced
- 2 tbsp sesame oil
- 1 tbsp honey
- 1 tbsp soy sauce
- 2 tbsp char siew sauce
- 2 tbsp minced ginger
- 2 tbsp hoisin sauce

Instructions:

1. Whisk together all marinade ingredients, in a small bowl. Coat the ribs well with the mixture. Place in a container with a lid, and refrigerate for 4 hours. Preheat the Ninja Air fryer to 330°F.
2. Place the ribs in the basket but do not throw away the liquid from the container. Cook for 40 minutes on Air Fry mode. Stir in the liquid, increase the temperature to 350 F, and cook for 10 more minutes.

French Beef

(Ready in about: 20 minutes | **Serves:** 2)

Ingredients:

- 7 oz. beef fillets; cut into strips
- 2 tsp. Provencal herbs
- ½ tbsp. mustard
- 1 tbsp. olive oil
- 1 green bell pepper; cut in strips
- 1 red onion; sliced
- Salt and black pepper to taste

Instructions:

1. Place all the ingredients in a baking dish that fits your air fryer and mix well.
2. Put the pan in the fryer and cook on air fryer mode at 400°F for 15 minutes. Divide the mixture between bowls and serve

Smoked Pork Roast

(Ready in about: 60 minutes | **Serves:** 4)

Ingredients:

- 2 lbs. pork loin roast
- 1 tsp. liquid smoke
- 1 tbsp. brown sugar
- 2 tbsp. oregano; chopped.
- 3 tbsp. smoked paprika
- 1 tbsp. olive oil
- Salt and black pepper to taste

Instructions:

1. Place all ingredients into a bowl, mix well and be sure the pork is thoroughly coated.
2. Transfer the roast to your air fryer and cook on air fryer mode at 370°F for 55 minutes. Slice the roast, divide it between plates and serve

Pork and Peanuts

(Ready in about: 20 minutes | **Serves:** 4)

Ingredients:

- 14 oz. pork chops; cubed
- 3 oz. peanuts; chopped.
- 7 oz. coconut milk
- 2 tsp. chili paste
- 1 tsp. coriander; ground
- 2 tbsp. olive oil
- 2 garlic cloves; minced
- 1 shallot; chopped.
- Salt and black pepper to taste

Instructions:

1. Place all of the ingredients into a pan that fits your air fryer; mix well
2. Put the pan in the fryer and cook on air fryer mode at 400°F for 15 minutes. Divide into bowls and serve.

Beef Roast

(Ready in about: 65 minutes | **Serves:** 4)

Ingredients:

- 2 lbs. beef roast
- 3 tbsp. olive oil
- 1 tbsp. smoked paprika
- 3 tbsp. garlic; minced
- Salt and black pepper to taste

Instructions:

1. In a bowl, combine all the ingredients and coat the roast well.
2. Place the roast in your air fryer and cook on air fryer mode at 390°F for 55 minutes. Slice the roast, divide it between plates and serve with a side salad

Basil Beef Roast

(Ready in about: 60 minutes | **Serves:** 6)

Ingredients:

- 1 cup beef stock
- 1 tbsp. basil; dried
- 1½ lbs. beef roast
- 2 garlic cloves; minced
- 2 carrots; sliced
- Salt and black pepper to taste

Instructions:

1. In a pan that fits your air fryer, combine all ingredients well.
2. Place the pan in the fryer and cook on air fryer mode at 390°F for 55 minutes
3. Slice the roast, divide it and the carrots between plates and serve with cooking juices drizzled on top.

Fish & Seafood Recipes

Parmesan Tilapia

(Ready in about: 15 minutes | **Serves:** 4)

Ingredients:

- ¾ cup grated Parmesan cheese
- 4 tilapia fillets
- 2 tsp paprika
- 1 tbsp olive oil
- 1 tbsp chopped parsley
- ¼ tsp garlic powder
- ¼ tsp salt

Instructions:

1. Preheat the Ninja Air fryer to 350°F. Mix parsley, Parmesan, garlic, salt, and paprika, in a shallow bowl.
2. Brush the olive oil over the fillets, and then coat them with the Parmesan mixture.
3. Place the tilapia onto a lined baking sheet, and then into the air fryer. Cook for about 4 to 5 minutes on all sides on Air Fry mode.

Cod and Lime Sauce

(Ready in about: 18 minutes | **Serves:** 4)

Ingredients:

- 4 cod fillets; boneless
- 2 tbsp. olive oil
- 3 tbsp. chives; chopped.
- 2 tsp. lime juice
- 3 tsp. lime zest
- 6 tbsp. butter; melted
- Salt and black pepper to taste

Instructions:

1. Season the fish with the salt and pepper, rub it with the oil and then put it in your air fryer.
2. Cook on air fryer mode at 360°F for 10 minutes, flipping once
3. Heat up a pan with the butter over medium heat and then add the chives, salt, pepper, lime juice and zest, whisk; cook for 1-2 minutes. Divide the fish between plates, drizzle the lime sauce all over and serve immediately

Salmon and Carrots

(Ready in about: 25 minutes | **Serves:** 2)

Ingredients:

- 2 salmon fillets; boneless
- ¼ cup veggie stock
- 1 tbsp. olive oil
- 1 cup baby carrots
- 3 garlic cloves; minced
- Salt and black pepper to taste

Instructions:

1. In your air fryer, mix all the ingredients.
2. Cook on air fryer mode at 370°F for 20 minutes. Divide everything between plates and serve

Chili Salmon Fillets

(Ready in about: 14 minutes | **Serves:** 2)

Ingredients:

- 2 salmon fillets; boneless
- 2 tbsp. garlic; minced
- 2 tbsp. olive oil
- 3 red chili peppers; chopped.
- 2 tbsp. lemon juice
- Salt and black pepper to taste

Instructions:

1. In a bowl, combine the ingredients, toss and coat fish well.
2. Transfer everything to your air fryer and cook on air fryer mode at 365°F for 8 minutes, flipping the fish halfway. Divide between plates and serve right away

Shrimp and Veggies

(Ready in about: 30 minutes | **Serves:** 4)

Ingredients:

- 1 lb. shrimp; peeled and deveined
- ½ cup red onion; chopped.
- 1 tbsp. butter; melted
- 1 tsp. sweet paprika
- 1 tsp. Worcestershire sauce
- 1 cup red bell pepper; chopped.
- 1 cup celery; chopped.
- Salt and black pepper to taste

Instructions:

1. Add all the ingredients to a bowl and mix well
2. Transfer everything to your air fryer and cook on air fryer mode 320°F for 20 minutes, shaking halfway. Divide between plates and serve

Tasty Pistachio Crusted Salmon

(Ready in about: 15 minutes | **Serves:** 1)

Ingredients:

- 1 salmon fillet
- 3 tbsp pistachios
- 1 tsp mustard
- 1 tsp lemon juice
- 1 tsp grated Parmesan cheese
- 1 tsp olive oil
- Pinch of garlic powder
- Pinch of sea salt
- Pinch of black pepper

Instructions:

1. Preheat the Ninja Air fryer to 350°F. Whisk the mustard and lemon juice together. Season the salmon with salt, pepper, and garlic powder. Brush the olive oil on all sides.
2. Brush the mustard-lemon mixture on top of the salmon. Chop the pistachios finely, and combine them with the Parmesan cheese.
3. Sprinkle them on top of the salmon. Place the salmon in the air fryer basket with the skin side down. Cook for 10 minutes on Air Fry mode.

Crab Cakes

(Ready in about: 55 minutes | **Serves:** 4)

Ingredients:

- ½ cup cooked crab meat
- ¼ cup chopped red onion
- ¼ cup chopped celery
- ¼ cup chopped red pepper
- Old Bay seasoning, as desired
- Zest of ½ lemon
- ¼ cup breadcrumbs
- 1 tbsp chopped basil
- 3 tbsp mayonnaise
- 2 tbsp chopped parsley
- Cooking spray

Instructions:

1. Preheat the Ninja Air fryer to 390°F. Place all ingredients in a large bowl and mix well until thoroughly incorporated.
2. Make 4 large crab cakes from the mixture and place on a lined sheet. Refrigerate for 30 minutes, to set.
3. Spay the air basket with cooking spray and arrange the crab cakes in it. Cook for 7 minutes on each side on Air Fry mode.

Cajun Salmon

(Ready in about: 10 minutes | **Serves:** 1)

Ingredients:

- 1 salmon fillet
- 2 lemon wedges
- Juice of ½ lemon
- 1 tbsp Cajun seasoning
- 1 tbsp chopped parsley, for garnishing
- ¼ tsp brown sugar

Instructions:

1. Preheat the Ninja Air fryer to 350°F. Meanwhile, combine the sugar and lemon and coat the salmon with this mixture thoroughly. Coat the salmon with the Cajun seasoning as well.
2. Place a parchment paper into the air fryer and cook the salmon for 7 minutes on Air Fry mode. If you use a thicker fillet, cook no more than 6 minutes. Serve with lemon wedges and chopped parsley.

Salmon Fillets

(Ready in about: 18 minutes | **Serves:** 4)

Ingredients:

- 4 salmon fillets; boneless
- 1 tsp. cumin; ground
- 1 tsp. garlic powder
- Juice of 1 lime
- 1 tsp. sweet paprika
- ½ tsp. chili powder
- 1 tbsp. olive oil
- Salt and black pepper to taste

Instructions:

1. In a bowl, mix the salmon with the other ingredients, rub / coat well and transfer to your air fryer.
2. Cook on air fryer mode at 350°F for 6 minutes on each side
3. Divide the fish between plates and serve right away with a side salad

Salmon and Orange Vinaigrette

(Ready in about: 15 minutes | **Serves:** 2)

Ingredients:
- 2 salmon fillets; boneless
- 2 tsp. honey
- 1 tbsp. dill; chopped.
- 2 tbsp. mustard
- 2 tbsp. olive oil
- 2 tbsp. parsley; chopped.
- A pinch of salt and black pepper
- Zest of ½ orange
- Juice of ½ orange

Instructions:
1. In a bowl, mix the orange zest with the orange juice, salt, pepper, mustard, honey, oil, dill and parsley and whisk well
2. Add the salmon to this mix, toss and transfer the fish to your air fryer
3. Cook on air fryer mode at 350°F for 10 minutes, flipping halfway. Divide the fish between plates, drizzle the orange vinaigrette all over and serve.

Rosemary Shrimp Kabobs

(Ready in about: 13 minutes | **Serves:** 2)

Ingredients:
- 8 shrimps; peeled and deveined
- 1 tbsp. rosemary; chopped.
- 1 tbsp. olive oil
- 8 red bell pepper slices
- 4 garlic cloves; minced
- Salt and black pepper to taste

Instructions:
1. Place all ingredients in a bowl and toss them well.
2. Thread 2 shrimp and 2 bell pepper slices on a skewer and then repeat with 2 more shrimp and bell pepper slices.
3. Thread another 2 shrimp and 2 bell pepper slices on the other skewer and then repeat with the last 2 shrimp and 2 bell pepper slices
4. Put the kabobs in your air fryer's basket., cook on air fryer mode at 360°F for 7 minutes and serve immediately with a side salad

Fish Sandwich

(Ready in about: 20 minutes | **Serves:** 4)

Ingredients:
- 2 oz breadcrumbs
- 10 capers
- 4 bread rolls
- 4 cod fillets
- 4 lettuce leaves
- 2 tbsp flour
- 4 tbsp pesto sauce
- Salt and pepper, to taste

Instructions:
1. Preheat the Ninja Air fryer to 370°F. Season the fillets with some salt and pepper, and coat them with the flour, and then dip in the breadcrumbs. You should get at the layer of breadcrumbs, that's why we don't use eggs for this recipe.

2. Arrange the fillets onto a baking mat. Cook for about 10 to 15 minutes on Air Fry mode. Cut the bread rolls in half.
3. Place a lettuce leaf on top of the bottom halves; place the fillets over. Spread a tbsp of pesto sauce on top of each fillet; top with the remaining halves.

Fried Salmon

(Ready in about: 13 minutes | **Serves:** 1)

Ingredients:
- 1 salmon fillet
- ¼ tsp garlic powder
- 1 tbsp soy sauce
- Salt and pepper

Instructions:
1. Preheat the Ninja Air fryer to 350°F. Combine the soy sauce with the garlic powder, salt, and pepper. Brush the mixture over the salmon.
2. Place the salmon onto a sheet of parchment paper and inside the air fryer. Cook for 10 minutes on Air Fry mode, until crispy on the outside and tender on the inside.

Clams and Potatoes

(Ready in about: 20 minutes | **Serves:** 4)

Ingredients:
- 1 lb. baby red potatoes; scrubbed
- 15 small clams; shucked
- 2 tbsp. cilantro; chopped.
- 10 oz. beer
- 2 chorizo links; sliced
- 1 yellow onion; chopped.
- 1 tsp. olive oil

Instructions:
1. In a pan that fits your air fryer, add all of the ingredients and toss
2. Place the pan in the fryer and cook on air fryer mode at 390°F for 15 minutes. Divide into bowls and serve.

Coconut Shrimp

(Ready in about: 30 minutes | **Serves:** 2)

Ingredients:
- 8 large shrimp
- 8 oz coconut milk
- ½ cup shredded coconut
- ½ cup breadcrumbs
- ½ cup orange jam
- 1 tbsp honey
- 1 tsp mustard
- ½ tsp cayenne pepper
- ¼ tsp hot sauce
- ¼ tsp salt
- ¼ tsp pepper

Instructions:
1. Preheat the Ninja Air fryer to 350°F. Combine the breadcrumbs, cayenne pepper, shredded coconut, salt, and pepper in a small bowl.
2. Dip the shrimp in the coconut milk, first, and then in the coconut crumbs. Arrange in the lined air fryer basket, and cook for 20 minutes on Air Fry mode.
3. Meanwhile whisk the jam, honey, hot sauce, and mustard. Serve the shrimp with the sauce.

Maple Salmon

(Ready in about: 15 minutes | **Serves:** 2)

Ingredients:
- 2 salmon fillets; boneless
- 1 tbsp. olive oil
- 2 tbsp. mustard
- 1 tbsp. maple syrup
- Salt and black pepper to taste

Instructions:
1. In a bowl, mix the mustard with the oil and the maple syrup; whisk well and brush the salmon with this mix.
2. Place the salmon in your air fryer and cook on air fryer mode at 370°F for 5 minutes on each side. Serve immediately with a side salad

Tuna Patties

(Ready in about: 50 minutes | **Serves:** 2)

Ingredients:
- 5 oz of canned tuna
- 1 small onion, diced
- 2 eggs
- ½ cup milk
- ¼ cup flour
- 1 tsp lime juice
- 1 tsp paprika
- 1 tsp chili powder, optional
- ½ tsp salt

Instructions:
1. Place all ingredients in a bowl, and mix to combine. Make two large patties, or a few smaller ones, out of the mixture
2. Place them on a lined sheet and refrigerate for 30 minutes. Preheat the Ninja Air fryer to 350°F. Cook the patties for about 6 minutes on each side on Roast mode.

Shrimp and Zucchini

(Ready in about: 18 minutes | **Serves:** 4)

Ingredients:
- 1 lb. shrimp; peeled and deveined
- 3 zucchinis; cut in medium chunks
- 2 tbsp. olive oil
- 1 tbsp. lemon juice
- 1 garlic clove; minced
- ½ cup parsley; chopped.
- ¼ cup tomato sauce
- 2 red onions; cut into chunks
- Salt and black pepper to taste

Instructions:
1. In a baking dish that fits your air fryer, mix all the ingredients except the parsley; toss well.
2. Place the baking dish into the fryer and cook on air fryer mode at 400°F for 8 minutes
3. Add the parsley and stir. Divide everything between plates and serve

Cod Cornflakes Nuggets

(Ready in about: 25 minutes | **Serves:** 4)

Ingredients:

- 1 ¼ lb. cod fillets, cut into chunks
- 1 egg
- 1 cup cornflakes
- ½ cup flour
- 1 tbsp water
- 1 tbsp olive oil
- Salt and pepper, to taste

Instructions:

1. Add the oil and cornflakes in a food processor, and process until crumbed. Season the fish chunks with salt and pepper. Beat the egg along with 1 tbsp water
2. Dredge the chunks in flour first, then dip in the egg, and coat with cornflakes. Arrange on a lined sheet. Cook at 350° for 15 minutes on Air Fry mode

Sides & Appetizers

Creamy Potatoes

(**Ready in about:** 25 minutes | **Serves:** 4)

Ingredients:
- 2 gold potatoes; cut into medium pieces
- 1 tbsp. olive oil
- 3 tbsp. sour cream
- Salt and black pepper to taste

Instructions:
1. In a baking dish that fits your air fryer, mix all the ingredients and toss.
2. Place the dish in the air fryer and cook on air fryer mode at 370°F for 20 minutes. Divide between plates and serve as a side dish

Steak and Minty Cheese

(**Ready in about:** 15 minutes | **Serves:** 4)

Ingredients:
- 2 New York strip steaks
- 8 oz halloumi cheese
- 12 kalamata olives
- Juice and zest of 1 lemon
- 2 tbsp chopped parsley
- 2 tbsp chopped mint
- Olive oil
- Salt and pepper, to taste

Instructions:
1. Preheat the Ninja Air fryer to 350°F. Season the steaks with salt and pepper, and gently brush with olive oil.
2. Place into the Air fryer and cook for 6 minutes (for medium rare) on Air Fry mode. When ready, remove to a plate and set aside
3. Drizzle the cheese with olive oil and place it in the Air fryer; cook for 4 minutes. Remove to a serving platter and serve with sliced steaks and olives, sprinkled with herbs, and lemon zest and juice

Tomato Bruschetta

(**Ready in about:** 15 minutes | **Serves:** 2)

Ingredients:
- 1 Italian Ciabatta Sandwich Bread
- 2 garlic cloves, minced
- 2 tomatoes, chopped
- 1 cup grated mozzarella cheese
- Olive oil to brush
- Basil leaves, chopped
- Salt and pepper to taste

Instructions:
1. Preheat your Ninja Air fryer to 380°F. Cut the bread in half, lengthways, then each piece again in half.
2. Drizzle each bit with olive oil and sprinkle with garlic. Top with the grated cheese, salt, and pepper
3. Place the bruschetta pieces into the air fryer basket and cook for 12 minutes on Air Fry mode
4. After 6 minutes, check for doneness. Once the air fryer beeps, remove the bruschetta to a serving platter, spoon over the tomatoes and chopped basil to serve.

Parmesan Cabbage Side Dish

(Ready in about: 30 minutes | **Serves:** 4)

Ingredients:
- ½ head of cabbage, cut into 4 wedges
- 2 cup Parmesan cheese
- 4 tbsp butter, melted
- 1 tsp smoked paprika
- Salt and pepper, to taste

Instructions:
1. Preheat the Ninja Air fryer to 330°F. Line the basket with parchment paper. Brush the butter over the cabbage wedges; season with salt and pepper
2. Coat the cabbage with the Parmesan cheese. Arrange in the basket and sprinkle with paprika.
3. Cook for 15 minutes on Air Fry mode, flip over and cook for an additional 10 minutes

Herby Fish Skewers

(Ready in about: 75 minutes | **Serves:** 4)

Ingredients;
- 1 lb. cod loin, boneless, skinless, cubed
- 1 lemon, cut in wedges to serve
- 1 tsp dill, chopped
- 1 tsp parsley, chopped
- 2 garlic cloves, grated
- 1 lemon, juiced and zested
- 3 tbsp olive oil
- Salt to taste

Instructions:
1. In a bowl, combine the olive oil, garlic, dill, parsley, salt, and lemon juice. Stir in the cod and place in the fridge to marinate for 1 hour
2. Preheat your Ninja Air fryer to 390°F. Thread the cod pieces onto halved skewers
3. Arrange into the oiled air fryer basket; cook for 10 minutes. Flip them over halfway through cooking. When ready, remove to a serving platter, scatter lemon zest and serve with wedges.

Turkey Scotch Eggs

(Ready in about: 20 minutes | **Serves:** 6)

Ingredients:
- 10 oz ground turkey
- ½ cup flour
- 2 garlic cloves, minced
- 2 eggs, lightly beaten
- 1 white onion, chopped
- 4 eggs, soft boiled, peeled
- ½ cup breadcrumbs
- 1 tsp dried mixed herbs
- Cooking spray
- Salt and pepper to taste

Instructions:
1. Mix together the onion, garlic, salt, and pepper. Shape into 4 balls. Wrap the turkey mixture around each egg, and ensure the eggs are well covered
2. Dust each egg ball in flour, then dip in the beaten eggs and finally roll in the crumbs, until coated. Spray with cooking spray. Lay the eggs into your Air fryer's basket
3. Set the temperature to 390°F and cook for 15 minutes. After 8 minutes, turn the eggs. Slice in half and serve warm.

Sweet Potato Side Salad

(Ready in about: 25 minutes | **Serves:** 2)

Ingredients:
- 2 sweet potatoes; peeled and cut into wedges
- 2 tbsp. avocado oil
- ¼ tsp. coriander; ground
- 4 tbsp. mayonnaise
- ½ tsp. curry powder
- ½ tsp. cumin; ground
- A pinch of cinnamon powder
- A pinch of ginger powder
- Salt and black pepper to taste

Instructions:
1. In your air fryer's basket, mix the sweet potato wedges with salt, pepper, coriander, curry powder and the oil; toss well.
2. Cook on air fryer mode at 370°F for 20 minutes, flipping them once
3. Transfer the potatoes to a bowl, then add the mayonnaise, cumin, ginger and the cinnamon. Toss and serve as a side salad

Eggplant Chips

(Ready in about: 20 minutes | **Serves:** 4)

Ingredients:
- 2 eggplants
- ⅓ cup cornstarch
- ½ cup water
- ⅓ cup olive oil
- 1 tsp dry thyme
- 2 tsp honey
- A pinch of salt

Instructions:
1. Preheat the Ninja Air fryer to 370°F. Cut the eggplants in slices of ½ -inch each. In a big bowl, mix the cornstarch, water, olive oil, and eggplant slices, until evenly coated
2. Line the air fryer basket with baking paper and spray with olive oil
3. Place the eggplants in the basket, scatter with thyme and cook for 15 minutes on Air Fry mode, shaking every 5 minutes. When ready, transfer the eggplants to a serving platter and drizzle with honey. Serve with yogurt dip.

Pork Bites

(Ready in about: 25 minutes | **Serves:** 4)

Ingredients:
- 1 lb. ground pork
- ¾ cup panko breadcrumbs
- ¾ cup coconut; shredded
- 2 tsp. garlic powder
- 2 eggs
- A drizzle of olive oil
- Salt and black pepper to taste

Instructions:
1. In a bowl, mix coconut with panko and stir well. In another bowl, mix the pork, salt, pepper, eggs and garlic powder and then shape medium meatballs out of this mix.
2. Dredge the meatballs in the coconut mix, place them in your air fryer's basket, introduce in the air fryer and cook on air fryer mode at 350°F for 15 minutes. Serve and enjoy!

Melt-in-the-Middle Meatballs

(Ready in about: 30 minutes | **Serves:** 6)

Ingredients:

- 2 lb. ground beef
- 2 eggs, beaten
- 1 potato, shredded
- ½ cup Parmesan cheese, grated
- 1 package cooked spaghetti to serve
- 2 cups tomato sauce to serve
- 2 tbsp chopped chives
- ¼ tsp pepper
- ½ tsp garlic powder
- ½ tsp salt
- Cooking spray
- Basil leaves to serve

Instructions:

1. Preheat the Ninja Air fryer to 330°F. In a large bowl, combine the potato, salt, pepper, garlic powder, eggs, and chives
2. Form 12 balls out of the mixture. Spray with cooking spray. Arrange half of the balls onto a lined air fryer basket
3. Cook for 14 minutes on Air Fry mode. After 7 minutes, turn the meatballs. Repeat with the other half. Serve over cooked spaghetti mixed with tomato sauce, sprinkled with Parmesan cheese and basil leaves.

Crispy Potato Fries

(Ready in about: 30 minutes | **Serves:** 4)

Ingredients:

- 4 russet potatoes, cut into sticks
- 2 garlic cloves, crushed
- 1 tsp fresh rosemary, chopped
- 2 tbsp butter, melted
- Salt and pepper, to taste

Instructions:

1. Add butter, garlic, salt, and pepper to a bowl; toss until the sticks are well-coated. Lay the potato sticks into the air fryer's basket. Cook for 15 minutes at 370 F. Shake the potatoes every 5 minutes
2. Once ready, check to ensure the fries are golden and crispy all over if not, return them to cook for a few minutes
3. Divide standing up between metal cups lined with nonstick baking paper, and serve sprinkled with rosemary.

Cauliflower Tater Tots

(Ready in about: 35 minutes | **Serves:** 10)

Ingredients:

- 2 lb. cauliflower florets, steamed
- 1 cup breadcrumbs
- 1 egg, beaten
- 5 oz cheddar cheese
- 1 onion, diced
- 1 tsp chopped oregano
- 1 tsp chopped chives
- 1 tsp garlic powder
- 1 tsp chopped parsley
- Salt and pepper, to taste

Instructions:

1. Mash the cauliflower and place it in a large bowl. Add the onion, parsley, oregano, chives, garlic powder, salt, and pepper, and cheddar cheese. Mix with hands until thoroughly combined
2. Form 12 balls out of the mixture. Line a baking sheet with paper. Dip half of the tater tots into the egg and then coat with breadcrumbs
3. Arrange them on the baking sheet and cook in the air fryer at 350°F for 15 minutes on Air Fry mode. Repeat with the other half.

Rosemary Mushrooms

(**Ready in about:** 20 minutes | **Serves:** 4)

Ingredients:
- 2 rosemary sprigs
- 3 garlic cloves, minced
- ¼ cup melted butter
- 12 oz button mushrooms
- ½ tsp salt
- ¼ tsp black pepper

Instructions:
1. Preheat the Ninja Air fryer to 350°F. Wash and pat dry the mushrooms and cut them in half. Place in a large bowl
2. Add the remaining ingredients to the bowl and toss well to combine. Transfer the mushrooms to the basket of the air fryer
3. Cook for 12 minutes on Air Fry mode, shaking once halfway through.

Fried Pin Wheels

(**Ready in about:** 50 minutes | **Serves:** 6)

Ingredients:
- 1 sheet puff pastry
- 1 ½ cups Gruyere cheese, grated
- 8 ham slices
- 4 tsp Dijon mustard

Instructions:
1. Preheat the Ninja air fryer to 370°F. Place the pastry on a lightly floured flat surface. Brush the mustard over and arrange the ham slices; top with cheese. Start at the shorter edge and roll up the pastry
2. Wrap it in a plastic foil and place in the freezer for about half an hour, until it becomes firm and comfortable to cut
3. Meanwhile, slice the pastry into 6 rounds. Line the air fryer basket with parchment paper, and arrange the pinwheels on top.
4. Cook for 10 minutes on Air Fry mode. Leave to cool on a wire rack before serving.

Citrus Cauliflower Mix

(Ready in about: 19 minutes | **Serves:** 4)

Ingredients:

- 2 small cauliflower heads; florets separated
- 4 tbsp. olive oil
- A pinch of hot pepper flakes
- Juice of 1 orange
- Salt and black pepper to taste

Instructions:

1. Brush the cauliflower with the oil, then season with salt, pepper and the pepper flakes
2. Transfer the cauliflower to your air fryer's basket and cook on air fryer mode at 380°F for 14 minutes
3. Divide between plates, drizzle orange juice all over and serve

Zesty Brussels Sprouts with Raisins

(Ready in about: 45 minutes | **Serves:** 4)

Ingredients:

- 14 oz Brussels sprouts, steamed.
- 2 oz toasted pine nuts
- 2 oz raisins
- 1 tbsp olive oil
- Juice and zest of 1 orange

Instructions:

1. Soak the raisins in the orange juice and let sit for about 20 minutes
2. Preheat the Ninja Air fryer to 370°F. Drizzle the Brussels sprouts with the olive oil, and place them in the basket of the air fryer. Cook for 15 minutes on Air Fry mode.
3. Remove to a bowl and top with pine nuts, raisins, and orange zest

Italian Mozzarella Sticks

(Ready in about: 18 minutes | **Serves:** 12)

Ingredients:

- 2 eggs; whisked
- 8 mozzarella cheese strings; halved.
- 1 tbsp. Italian seasoning
- 1 cup parmesan cheese; grated
- A drizzle of olive oil
- Salt and black pepper to taste

Instructions:

1. In a bowl, mix the parmesan, salt, pepper and Italian seasoning; stir. Put the whisked eggs in another bowl.
2. Dip the mozzarella sticks in the egg mixture, then in the parmesan mix
3. Dip the sticks one more time in egg and parmesan and place them in your air fryer's basket. Drizzle the oil over them and cook on air fryer mode at 390°F for 8 minutes, flipping them halfway. Serve as an appetizer

Wrapped Asparagus in Bacon

(**Ready in about:** 30 minutes | **Serves:** 6)

Ingredients:
- 1 lb. asparagus spears, trimmed.
- ½ cup Parmesan cheese, grated.
- 1 lb. bacon, sliced
- Cooking spray
- Salt and pepper, to taste

Instructions:
1. Preheat the Ninja Air fryer to 370 F. Place the bacon slices out on a work surface, top each one with one asparagus spear and half of the cheese. Wrap the bacon around the asparagus
2. Line the air fryer basket with parchment paper. Arrange the wraps into the basket, scatter over the remaining cheese, season with salt and black pepper, and spray with cooking spray
3. Cook for 8 to 10 minutes on Roast mode. If necessary, work in batches. Serve hot!

Basil and Cilantro Crackers

(**Ready in about:** 26 minutes | **Serves:** 6)

Ingredients:
- 1¼ cups flour
- 4 tbsp. butter; melted
- 2 tbsp. basil; minced
- ½ tsp. baking powder
- 1 garlic clove; minced
- 2 tbsp. cilantro; minced
- Salt and black pepper to taste

Instructions:
1. Add all of the ingredients to a bowl and stir until you obtain a dough
2. Spread this on a lined baking sheet that fits your air fryer. Place the baking sheet in the fryer at 325°F and cook for 16 minutes on air fryer mode. Cool down, cut and serve.

Zucchini Balls

(**Ready in about:** 22 minutes | **Serves:** 8)

Ingredients:
- 3 zucchinis; grated
- ½ cup dill; chopped.
- 1 egg
- ½ cup white flour
- 2 garlic cloves; minced.
- Cooking spray
- Salt and black pepper to taste

Instructions:
1. In a bowl, mix all the ingredients and stir. Shape the mix into medium balls and place them into your air fryer's basket.
2. Cook on air fryer mode at 375°F for 12 minutes, flipping them halfway. Serve them as a snack right away

Herbed Potatoes

(Ready in about: 40 minutes | **Serves:** 4)

Ingredients:

- 3 large potatoes; peeled and cut into chunks
- 2 tbsp. olive oil
- 1 tsp. parsley; chopped.
- 1 tsp. chives; chopped.
- 1 tsp. oregano; chopped.
- 1 tbsp. garlic; minced
- Salt and black pepper to taste

Instructions:

1. Mix all of the ingredients in your air fryer and stir well. Cook on air fryer mode at 370°F for 30 minutes. Divide between plates and serve as a side dish.

French Carrots

(Ready in about: 25 minutes | **Serves:** 4)

Ingredients:

- 1 lb. baby carrots; trimmed.
- 2 tsp. olive oil
- 2 tbsp. lime juice
- 1 tsp. herbs de Provence

Instructions:

1. In a bowl, mix all ingredients well and then transfer to your air fryer's basket
2. Cook on air fryer mode at 320°F for 20 minutes. Divide between plates and serve as a side dish

Cumin Baby Carrots

(Ready in about: 25 minutes | **Serves:** 4)

Ingredients:

- 1 ¼ lb. baby carrots
- 1 handful cilantro, chopped.
- 2 tbsp olive oil
- ½ tsp cumin powder
- ½ tsp garlic powder
- 1 tsp cumin seeds
- 1 tsp salt
- ½ tsp black pepper

Instructions:

1. Preheat the Ninja Air fryer to 370°F. Place the baby carrots in a large bowl. Add cumin seeds, cumin, olive oil, salt, garlic powder, and pepper, and stir to coat them well
2. Put the carrots in the air fryer's basket, and cook for 20 minutes on Roast mode
3. Remove to a platter and sprinkle with chopped cilantro, to serve.

Vegetarian Recipes

Quinoa Stuffed Peppers

(**Ready in about:** 16 minutes | **Serves:** 1)

Ingredients:

- ¼ cup cooked quinoa
- ½ diced tomato, plus one tomato slice
- 1 bell pepper
- ½ tbsp diced onion
- 1 tsp olive oil
- ¼ tsp dried basil
- ¼ tsp smoked paprika
- Salt and pepper, to taste

Instructions:

1. Preheat the Ninja Air fryer to 350°F. Core and clean the bell pepper to prepare it for stuffing. Brush the pepper with half of the olive oil on the outside
2. In a small bowl, combine all of the other ingredients, except the tomato slice and reserved half-teaspoon olive oil
3. Stuff the pepper with the filling. Top with the tomato slice. Brush the tomato slice with the remaining half-teaspoon of olive oil and sprinkle with basil. Cook for 10 minutes on Air Fry mode.

Crispy Nachos

(**Ready in about:** 20 minutes | **Serves:** 2)

Ingredients:

- 1 cup sweet corn
- ½ tsp chili powder
- 1 cup all-purpose flour
- 2 to 3 tbsp water
- 1 tbsp butter
- Salt to taste

Instructions:

1. Add a small amount of water to the sweet corn and grind until you obtain an excellent paste. In a large bowl, add the flour, the salt, the chili powder, the butter and mix very well. Add the corn and stir well
2. Start to knead with your palm until you obtain a stiff dough. Preheat the air fryer to 350°F
3. Meanwhile, dust a little bit of flour and spread the batter with a rolling pin. Make it around ½ inch thick. Cut it in any shape you want and cook in the Air Fryer for 10 minutes on Air Fry mode. Serve with guacamole salsa.

Fried Ravioli

(**Ready in about:** 15 minutes | **Serves:** 6)

Ingredients:

- 1 package cheese ravioli
- ¼ cup Parmesan cheese
- 2 cup Italian breadcrumbs
- 1 tsp olive oil
- 1 cup buttermilk
- ¼ tsp garlic powder

Instructions:

1. Preheat the Ninja Air fryer to 390°F. In a bowl, combine the crumbs, Parmesan cheese, garlic powder, and olive oil

2. Dip the ravioli in the buttermilk and then coat them with the breadcrumb mixture. Line a baking sheet with parchment paper and arrange the ravioli on it
3. Place in the air fryer and cook for 5 minutes on Air Fry mode. Serve the air-fried ravioli with marinara jar sauce.

Avocado Rolls

(Ready in about: 15 minutes | **Serves:** 5)

Ingredients:

- 3 avocados, pitted and peeled
- 10 egg roll wrappers
- 1 tomato, diced
- ¼ tsp pepper
- ½ tsp salt

Instructions:

1. Place all filling ingredients in a bowl. Mash with a fork until somewhat smooth
2. Divide the feeling between the egg wrappers. Wet your finger and brush along the edges so the wrappers can seal well. Roll and seal the wrappers.
3. Arrange them on the lined air fryer basket, and place into the air fryer. Cook at 350°F, for 5 minutes on Air Fry mode. Serve with chili dipping and enjoy.

Pasta and Roasted Veggies

(Ready in about: 25 minutes | **Serves:** 6)

Ingredients:

- 1 lb. penne, cooked
- ½ cup kalamata olives, pitted, halved.
- ¼ cup olive oil
- 1 cup grape tomatoes, halved
- 4 oz mushrooms, sliced
- 1 pepper, sliced
- 1 acorn squash, sliced
- 1 zucchini, sliced
- 3 tbsp balsamic vinegar
- 2 tbsp chopped basil
- 1 tsp Italian seasoning
- Salt and pepper, to taste

Instructions:

1. Preheat the Ninja Air fryer to 380°F. Combine the pepper, zucchini, squash, mushrooms, and olive oil, in a large bowl
2. Season with salt and pepper. Cook the veggies for 15 minutes on Air Fry mode. In a large bowl, combine the penne, roasted vegetables, olives, tomatoes, Italian seasoning, and vinegar. Sprinkle basil and serve

Prawn Toast

(Ready in about: 12 minutes | **Serves:** 2)

Ingredients:

- 1 large spring onion, finely sliced
- 6 large prawns, shells removed, chopped.
- ½ cup sweet corn
- 1 egg white, whisked
- 3 white slices of bread
- 1 tbsp black sesame seeds

Instructions:

1. In a bowl, place the prawns, corn, spring onion and the black sesame seeds

2. Add the whisked egg white, and mix the ingredients. Spread the mixture over the bread slices.
3. Place the prawns in the Air Fryer's basket and sprinkle with oil. Fry the prawns until golden, for 8-10 minutes at 370° F on Air Fry mode. Serve with ketchup or chili sauce

Baby Porcupine Meatballs

(**Ready in about:** 30 minutes | **Serves:** 4)

Ingredients:
- 1 lb. of ground beef
- 1 garlic clove, minced
- 1 cup rice
- 2 cups of tomato juice
- 1 onion, chopped
- 1 green bell pepper, finely chopped.
- 2 tbsp Worcestershire sauce
- 1 tsp celery salt
- 1 tsp oregano

Instructions:
1. Combine the rice, ground beef, onion, celery, salt, green peppers, and garlic. Shape into balls of 1 inch each. Arrange the balls in the basket of the Air Fryer. Cook for 15 minutes at 320°F. After 8 minutes, shape the balls
2. Heat the tomato juice, cloves, oregano, and Worcestershire sauce in a saucepan over medium heat. Pour in the meatballs, bring to a boil, reduce the heat and simmer for 10 minutes, stirring often. Serve warm.

Vegetable Tortilla Pizza

(**Ready in about:** 15 minutes | **Serves:** 1)

Ingredients:
- 4 zucchini slices
- 4 eggplant slices
- 4 red onion Rings
- ½ green bell pepper, chopped.
- ¼ cup grated cheddar cheese
- ¼ cup grated mozzarella cheese
- 3 cherry tomatoes, quartered
- 1 tortilla
- 1 ½ tbsp tomato paste
- 1 tbsp cooked sweet corn
- ¼ tsp basil
- ¼ tsp oregano

Instructions:
1. Preheat the Ninja Air fryer to 350°F. Spread the tomato paste on the tortilla. Arrange the zucchini and eggplant slices first, then green peppers, and onion rings
2. Lay the cherry tomatoes and sprinkle the sweet corn over. Sprinkle with oregano and basil. Top with cheddar and mozzarella. Place in the air fryer and cook for 10 minutes on Air Fry mode.

Tofu Sandwich

(**Ready in about:** 20 minutes | **Serves:** 1)

Ingredients:
- 2 slices of bread
- ¼ cup red cabbage, shredded.
- 1-inch thick Tofu slice
- ¼ tsp vinegar
- 2 tsp olive oil divided
- Salt and pepper, to taste

Instructions:

1. Preheat the Ninja Air fryer to 350°F. Place the bread slices and toast for 3 minutes on Roast mode; set aside. Brush the tofu with 1 tsp of oil, and place in the basket of the air fryer. Bake for 5 minutes on each side on Roast mode
2. Combine the cabbage, remaining oil, and vinegar, and season with salt and pepper. Place the tofu on top of one bread slice, place the cabbage over, and top with the other bread slice.

Veggie Skewers

(Ready in about: 20 minutes | **Serves:** 4)

Ingredients:

- 2 boiled and mashed potatoes
- ⅔ cup canned beans
- ⅓ cup grated carrots
- ¼ cup chopped fresh mint leaves
- ½ cup paneer
- 1 green chili
- 1-inch piece of fresh ginger
- 3 garlic cloves
- 2 tbsp corn flour
- ½ tsp garam masala powder
- Salt, to taste

Instructions:

1. Soak 12 skewers until ready to use. Preheat the Ninja Air fryer to 390°F. Place the beans, carrots, garlic, ginger, chili, paneer, and mint, in a food processor and process until smooth; transfer to a bowl
2. Add the mashed potatoes, corn flour, some salt, and garam masala powder to the bowl. Mix until fully incorporated
3. Divide the mixture into 12 equal pieces. Shape each of the pieces around a skewer. Cook the skewers for 10 minutes on Air Fry mode.

Roasted Vegetable Salad

(Ready in about: 25 minutes | **Serves:** 1)

Ingredients:

- 1 potato, peeled and chopped.
- ½ small beetroot, sliced
- 1 cup cherry tomatoes
- ¼ onion, sliced
- ½ tsp cumin
- ½ tsp turmeric
- ¼ tsp sea salt
- 1 carrot, sliced diagonally
- Juice of 1 lemon
- A handful of rocket salad
- A handful of baby spinach
- 3 tbsp canned chickpeas
- 2 tbsp olive oil
- Parmesan shavings

Instructions:

1. Preheat the Ninja Air fryer to 370°F. Combine the onion, potato, cherry tomatoes, carrot, beetroot, cumin, seas salt, turmeric, and 1 tbsp olive oil, in a bowl
2. Place in the air fryer and cook for 20 minutes on Air Fry mode; let cool for 2 minutes
3. Place the rocket, salad, spinach, lemon juice, and 1 tbsp olive oil, into a serving bowl. Mix to combine; stir in the roasted veggies. Top with chickpeas and Parmesan shavings.

Asian Style Paneer Cutlet

(Ready in about: 15 minutes | **Serves:** 1)

Ingredients:

- 1 small onion, finely chopped.
- 1 cup grated cheese
- 2 cup grated paneer
- ½ tsp chai masala
- ½ tsp oregano
- 1 tsp butter
- ½ tsp garlic powder
- ½ tsp salt

Instructions:

1. Preheat the Ninja Air fryer to 350°F. Oil the air fryer basket. Mix all ingredients in a bowl, until well incorporated
2. Make cutlets out of the mixture and place them on the greased baking dish. Place the baking dish in the air fryer and cook the cutlets for 10 minutes

Crispy Cheese Lings

(Ready in about: 15 minutes | **Serves:** 4)

Ingredients:

- 4 cups grated cheddar cheese
- 1 cup all-purpose flour
- 1 tbsp baking powder
- ¼ tsp chili powder
- 1-2 tbsp water
- 1 tbsp butter
- ¼ tsp salt, to taste

Instructions:

1. Mix the flour and the baking powder. Add the chili powder, salt, butter, cheese and 1-2 tbsp of water to the mixture. Make a stiff dough. Knead the dough for a while
2. Sprinkle a tbsp or so of flour on the table. Take a rolling pin and roll the dough into ½ -inch thickness.
3. Cut the dough in any shape you want. Fry the cheese lings for 6 minutes at 370°F on Air Fry mode

Sweet Potato Skewers

(Ready in about: 20 minutes | **Serves:** 1)

Ingredients:

- 1 large sweet potato
- 1 green bell pepper
- 1 beetroot
- 1 tbsp olive oil
- ½ tsp turmeric
- ¼ tsp garlic powder
- 1 tsp chili flakes
- ¼ tsp black pepper
- ¼ tsp paprika

Instructions:

1. Soak 3 to 4 skewers until ready to use. Preheat the Ninja Air fryer to 350°F. Peel the veggies and cut them into bite-sized chunks
2. Place the chunks in a bowl along with the remaining ingredients. Mix until fully coated. Thread the veggies in this order: potato, pepper, beetroot
3. Place in the air fryer and cook for 15 minutes on Air Fry mode; flip skewers halfway through.

Delicious Potato Filled Bread Rolls

(Ready in about: 25 minutes | **Serves:** 4)

Ingredients:

- 8 slices of bread
- 2 green chilies, deseeded, chopped.
- 1 medium onion, chopped.
- ½ tsp turmeric
- ½ tsp mustard seeds
- 2 sprigs curry leaf
- 5 large potatoes, boiled, mashed
- 1 tbsp olive oil
- Salt, to taste

Instructions:

1. Preheat the Ninja Air fryer to 350°F. Combine the olive oil, onion, curry leaves, and mustard seed, in the air fryer basket. Cook for 5 minutes
2. Mix the onion mixture with the mashed potatoes, chilies, turmeric, and some salt. Divide the dough into 8 equal pieces
3. Trim the sides of the bread, and wet it with some water. Make sure to get rid of the excess water. Take one wet bread slice in your palm and place one of the potato pieces in the center.
4. Roll the bread over the filling, sealing the edges. Place the rolls onto a prepared baking dish, and cook for 12 minutes on Air Fry mode.

Pineapple Appetizer Ribs

(Ready in about: 30 minutes | **Serves:** 4)

Ingredients:

- 2 lb. cut spareribs
- 5 oz canned pineapple juice
- 2 cups water
- 7 oz salad dressing
- Garlic salt
- Salt and black pepper

Instructions:

1. Sprinkle the ribs with salt and pepper and place them in a saucepan. Pour water and cook the ribs for around 12 minutes on high heat
2. Drain the ribs and arrange them in the Air Fryer. Sprinkle with garlic salt. Cook for 15 minutes at 390°F on Air Fry mode
3. Meanwhile, prepare the sauce by combining the salad dressing and the pineapple juice. Serve the ribs with this delicious dressing sauce!

Crispy Kale Chips

(Ready in about: 9 minutes | **Serves:** 2)

Ingredients:

- 4 cups kale, stemmed and packed.
- 1 tsp of vegan seasoning
- 1 tbsp of yeast flakes
- 2 tbsp of olive oil
- Salt to taste

Instructions:

1. In a bowl, add the oil, the kale, the vegan seasoning, and the yeast and mix well
2. Dump the coated kale in the Air Fryer's basket. Set the heat to 370°F and fry for a total of 6 minutes on Air Fry mode. Shake it from time to time.

Tomato Stuffed Squash

(Ready in about: 50 minutes | **Serves:** 3)

Ingredients:
- 6 grape tomatoes, halved.
- ½ butternut squash
- 1 poblano pepper, cut into strips
- ¼ cup grated mozzarella, optional
- 2 tsp olive oil divided
- Salt and pepper, to taste

Instructions:
1. Preheat the Ninja Air fryer to 350°F. Meanwhile, cut trim the ends and cut the squash lengthwise. You will only need one half for this recipe
2. Scoop the flash out, so you make room for the filling. Brush 1 tsp oil over the squash. Place in the Air fryer and roast for 30 minutes.
3. Combine the other teaspoon of olive oil with the tomatoes and poblanos. Season with salt and pepper, to taste. Place the peppers and tomatoes into the squash. Cook for 15 more minutes on Air Fry mode. If using mozzarella, add it on top of the squash, two minutes before the end

Cheese Balls

(Ready in about: 12 minutes | **Serves:** 2)

Ingredients:
- 2 oz paneer cheese
- 1 green chili, chopped
- 2 medium onions, chopped.
- 2 tbsp flour
- 1 tbsp olive oil
- 1 tbsp corn flour
- a few leaves of coriander, chopped.
- 1-inch ginger piece, chopped
- 1 tsp red chili powder
- Salt to taste

Instructions:
1. Mix all ingredients, except the oil and the cheese. Take a small part of the mixture, roll it up and slowly press to flatten it
2. Stuff in 1 cube of cheese and seal the edges. Repeat with the rest of the mixture. Fry the balls in the Air Fryer for 12 minutes on Air Fry mode and at 370° F. Serve hot, with ketchup.

Dessert Recipes

Pineapple Cake

(Ready in about: 50 minutes | **Serves:** 4)

Ingredients:
- 2 oz dark chocolate, grated.
- 8 oz self-rising flour
- 4 oz butter
- 7 oz pineapple chunks
- 1 egg
- ½ cup sugar
- ½ cup pineapple juice
- 2 tbsp milk

Instructions:
1. Preheat the Ninja Air fryer to 390°F. Place the butter and flour into a bowl and rub the mixture with your fingers until crumbed. Stir in the pineapple, sugar, chocolate, and juice
2. Beat the eggs and milk separately, and then add them to the batter. Transfer the batter to a previously prepared (greased or lined) cake pan, and cook for 40 minutes on Roast mode. Let cool for at least 10 minutes before serving.

Chocolaty Fudge

(Ready in about: 55 minutes | **Serves:** 8)

Ingredients:
- 1 cup sugar
- 7 oz flour, sifted
- 4 oz butter
- 1 oz cocoa powder
- ¼ cup milk
- 1 orange, juice and zest
- 2 eggs
- 1 tbsp honey
- 1 tsp vanilla extract

Icing:
- 4 oz powdered sugar
- 1 oz butter, melted
- 1 tbsp milk
- 1 tbsp brown sugar
- 2 tsp honey

Instructions:
1. Preheat the Ninja Air fryer to 350°F. In a bowl, mix the dry ingredients for the fudge. Mix the wet ingredients separately. Combine the two mixtures gently.
2. Transfer the batter to a prepared air fryer basket. Cook for about 35 minutes on Roast mode. Once the timer beeps, check to ensure the cake is cooked
3. For the Topping whisk together all of the icing ingredients. When the cake is cooled, coat it with the icing. Let set before slicing the fudge

Passion Fruit Pudding Recipe

(**Ready in about:** 50 Minutes | **Serves:** 6)

Ingredients:
- 1 cup Paleo passion fruit curd.
- 3 ½-ounce almond milk
- 3 ½-ounce maple syrup
- 3 eggs
- 2-ounce ghee; melted
- ½ cup almond flour
- 4 passion fruits; pulp and seeds
- ½ tsp baking powder

Instructions:
1. In a bowl; mix the half of the fruit curd with passion fruit seeds and pulp; stir and divide into 6 heat proof ramekins
2. In a bowl; whisked eggs with maple syrup, ghee, the rest of the curd, baking powder, milk and flour and stir well.
3. Divide this into the ramekins as well, introduce in the fryer and cook at 200°F, for 40 minutes. Leave puddings to cool down and serve!

Lime Tapioca Pudding

(**Ready in about:** 25 minutes | **Serves:** 6)

Ingredients:
- ⅓ cup tapioca pearls; rinsed.
- ½ cup sugar
- 2 cups milk
- Zest of 1 lime

Instructions:
1. Place all ingredients in a heat-proof dish that fits your air fryer; whisk well
2. Put the dish in the fryer and cook at 320°F for 15 minutes. Set the pudding aside for 10 minutes, divide into bowls and serve

Chocolate Soufflé

(**Ready in about:** 25 minutes | **Serves:** 2)

Ingredients:
- 3 oz chocolate, melted
- ¼ cup butter, melted
- 2 eggs, whites and yolks separated.
- 3 tbsp sugar
- 2 tbsp flour
- ½ tsp vanilla extract

Instructions:
1. Beat the yolks along with the sugar and vanilla extract. Stir in butter, chocolate, and flour. Preheat the Ninja Air fryer to 330°F. Whisk the whites until a stiff peak forms.
2. Working in batches, gently combine the egg whites with the chocolate mixture. Divide the batter between two greased ramekins. Cook for 14 minutes on Roast.

Pineapple and Carrot Cake

(Ready in about: 55 minutes | **Serves:** 6)

Ingredients:

- 5 oz. flour
- ¼ cup pineapple juice
- ⅓ cup carrots; grated
- ⅓ cup coconut flakes; shredded.
- ½ cup sugar
- 1 egg; whisked
- 3 tbsp. yogurt
- 4 tbsp. vegetable oil
- ¾ tsp. baking powder
- ½ tsp. baking soda
- ½ tsp. cinnamon powder
- Cooking spray

Instructions:

1. Place all of the ingredients (except the cooking spray) in a bowl and mix well.
2. Pour the mixture into a spring form pan, greased with cooking spray, that fits your air fryer
3. Place the pan in your air fryer and cook at 320°F for 45 minutes. Allow the cake to cool before cutting and serving

Fried Doughnuts

(Ready in about: 25 minutes | **Serves:** 4)

Ingredients:

- 8 oz self-rising flour
- 2 oz brown sugar
- 1 egg
- ½ cup milk
- 1 tsp baking powder
- 2 ½ tbsp butter

Instructions:

1. Preheat the Ninja Air fryer to 350°F. Beat the butter with the sugar, until smooth; beat in eggs, and milk. In a bowl, combine the flour with the baking powder.
2. Gently fold the flour into the butter mixture. Form donut shapes and cut off the center with cookie cutters. Arrange on a lined baking sheet and cook in the Air fryer for 15 minutes on Air Fry mode. Serve with whipped cream.

Yummy Blueberry Muffins

(Ready in about: 30 minutes | **Serves:** 10)

Ingredients:

- 1 ½ cup flour
- ¼ cup vegetable oil
- 1 cup blueberries
- ½ cup sugar
- 1 egg
- 2 tsp vanilla extract
- 2 tsp baking powder
- ½ tsp salt
- Yogurt, as needed

Instructions:

1. Preheat the Ninja Air fryer to 350°F. Combine all the flour, salt and baking powder in a bowl.
2. In a bowl, place the oil, vanilla extract, and egg. Fill the rest of the bowl with yogurt. Whisk the mixture until fully incorporated. Combine the wet and dry ingredients
3. Gently fold in the blueberries. Divide the mixture between 10 muffin cups. You may need to cook in batches. Cook for 10 minutes on Air Fry mode, until nice and crispy.

Chocolate Chip Cookies

(Ready in about: 30 minutes | **Serves:** 8)

Ingredients:
- 6 oz self-rising flour
- 4 oz butter
- 2 oz white chocolate chips
- 3 oz brown sugar
- 1 tbsp honey
- 1 ½ tbsp milk

Instructions:
1. Preheat the Ninja Air fryer to 350°F. Beat the butter and sugar until fluffy. Then, beat in the honey, milk, and flour. Gently fold in the chocolate chips
2. Drop spoonfuls of the mixture onto a prepared cookie sheet. Cook for 18 minutes on Air Fry mode. Once the timer beeps, make sure the cookies are just set.

Strawberry Cream

(Ready in about: 20 minutes | **Serves:** 6)

Ingredients:
- 8 oz. cream cheese
- 4 oz. strawberries
- ½ cup heavy cream
- 2 tbsp. water
- ½ tbsp. lemon juice
- 1 tsp. gelatin
- ¼ tsp. sugar

Instructions:
1. Place all ingredients in your blender and pulse
2. Divide the mixture into 6 ramekins and place them in your air fryer
3. Cook at 330°F for 15 minutes. Refrigerate (or place briefly in freezer) and serve the cream really cold.

Filled Coconut and Oat Cookies

(Ready in about: 30 minutes | **Serves:** 4)

Ingredients:
- ½ cup oats
- 1 small egg, beaten
- ¼ cup coconut flakes
- 3 oz sugar
- 5 ½ oz flour
- 1 tsp vanilla extract

Filling:
- 1 oz white chocolate, melted.
- 4 oz powdered sugar
- 2 oz butter
- 1 tsp vanilla extract

Instructions:
1. Beat all cookie ingredients, with an electric mixer, except the flour. When smooth, fold in the flour. Drop spoonfuls of the batter onto a prepared cookie sheet
2. Cook in the Air fryer at 350°F for about 18 minutes on Air Fry mode; let cool. Meanwhile, prepare the filling by beating all ingredients together. Spread the mixture on half of the cookies. Top with the other halves to make cookie sandwiches

Lime Muffins

(Ready in about: 30 minutes | **Serves:** 6)

Ingredients:

- 2 eggs plus 1 yolk
- 1 cup yogurt
- ¼ cup superfine sugar
- 8 oz cream cheese
- Juice and zest of 2 limes
- 1 tsp vanilla extract

Instructions:

1. Preheat the Ninja Air fryer to 330°F. With a spatula, gently combine the yogurt and cheese.
2. In another bowl, beat together the rest of the ingredients. Gently fold the lime with the cheese mixture. Divide the batter between 6 lined muffin tins. Cook in the Air fryer for 10 minutes on Air Fry mode

Apple Pie

(Ready in about: 30 minutes | **Serves:** 9)

Ingredients:

- 4 apples, diced
- 1 egg, beaten
- 3 large puff pastry sheets
- 2 oz sugar
- 1 oz brown sugar
- 2 oz butter, melted
- 2 tsp cinnamon
- ¼ tsp salt

Instructions:

1. Whisk the white sugar, brown sugar, cinnamon, salt, and butter together. Place the apples in a baking dish and coat them with the mixture.
2. Slide the dish into the Air fryer and cook for 10 minutes on Roast mode at 350 F. Meanwhile, roll out the pastry on a floured flat surface, and cut each sheet into 6 equal pieces. Divide the apple filling between the parts
3. Brush the edges of the pastry squares with the egg. Fold and seal the edges with a fork. Place on a lined baking sheet and cook in the fryer at 350°F for 8 minutes on Roast mode. Flip them over, increase the temperature to 390 F, and cook for 2 more minutes

Molten Lava Cake

(Ready in about: 20 minutes | **Serves:** 4)

Ingredients:

- 3 ½ oz butter, melted
- 3 ½ oz dark chocolate, melted.
- 2 eggs
- 3 ½ tbsp sugar
- 1 ½ tbsp self-rising flour

Instructions:

1. Grease 4 ramekins with butter. Preheat the Ninja Air fryer to 375°F. Beat the eggs and sugar until frothy. Stir in the butter and chocolate.
2. Gently fold in the flour. Divide the mixture between the ramekins and bake in the air fryer for 10 minutes on Air Fry mode. Let cool for 2 minutes before turning the lava cakes upside down onto serving plates

Fried Snickerdoodle Poppers

(Ready in about: 30 minutes | **Serves:** 6)

Ingredients:
- 1 can of Pillsbury Grands Flaky Layers Biscuits
- 1 ½ cups cinnamon sugar
- 1 box instant vanilla Jell-O
- Melted butter, for brushing

Instructions:
1. Preheat the Ninja Air fryer to 350°F. Unroll the flaky biscuits and cut them into fourths. Roll each ¼ into a ball.
2. Arrange the balls on a lined baking sheet, and cook in the Air fryer for 7 minutes, or until golden, on Air Fry mode.
3. Meanwhile, prepare the Jell-O following the package's instructions. Using an injector, inject some of the vanilla pudding into each ball
4. Brush the balls with melted butter and then coat them with cinnamon sugar.

Pumpkin Cake

(Ready in about: 35 minutes | **Serves:** 8)

Ingredients:
- 8 oz. canned pumpkin puree
- ½ cup Greek yogurt
- 1 egg; whisked
- ¾ cup sugar
- 1 cup white flour
- 1 tsp. baking powder
- ¾ tsp. pumpkin pie spice
- Cooking spray

Instructions:
1. Place all ingredients (other than the cooking spray) in a bowl and mix well
2. Grease a cake pan with cooking spray, pour the cake batter inside and spread
3. Place the pan in the air fryer and cook at 330°F for 25 minutes. Let the cake cool down, slice and serve.

Coffee Cheesecakes Recipe

(Ready in about: 30 Minutes | **Serves:** 6)

Ingredients:

For the cheesecakes:
- 2 tbsp butter
- 8-ounce cream cheese
- 3 tbsp coffee
- 3 eggs
- ⅓ cup sugar
- 1 tbsp caramel syrup

For the frosting:
- 3 tbsp caramel syrup
- 2 tbsp sugar
- 3 tbsp butter
- 8-ounce mascarpone cheese; soft

Instructions:

1. In your blender, mix cream cheese with eggs, 2 tablespoon butter, coffee, 1 tablespoon caramel syrup and ⅓ cup sugar and pulse very well, spoon into a cupcakes pan that fits your air fryer, introduce in the fryer and cook at 320°F and bake for 20 minutes
2. Leave aside to cool down and then keep in the freezer for 3 hours. Meanwhile; in a bowl, mix 3 tablespoon butter with 3 tablespoon caramel syrup, 2 tablespoon sugar and mascarpone, blend well, spoon this over cheesecakes and serve them

Tangerine Cake Recipe

(Ready in about: 30 Minutes | **Serves:** 8)

Ingredients:

- 2 cups flour
- ½ tsp vanilla extract
- ¼ cup olive oil
- ½ cup milk
- ¾ cup sugar
- 1 tsp cider vinegar
- Juice and zest from 2 lemons
- Juice and zest from 1 tangerine
- Tangerine segments; for serving

Instructions:

1. In a bowl; mix flour with sugar and stir
2. In another bowl, mix oil with milk, vinegar, vanilla extract, lemon juice and zest and tangerine zest and whisk very well
3. Add flour; stir well, pour this into a cake pan that fits your air fryer, introduce in the fryer and cook at 360°F, for 20 minutes. Serve right away with tangerine segments on top

Apple Jam

(Ready in about: 30 minutes | **Serves:** 8)

Ingredients:

- 8 apples; peeled, cored and blended.
- 1 tsp. cinnamon powder
- 1 cup apple juice

Instructions:

1. In a pan that fits your air fryer, mix the apples with the cinnamon and apple juice; stir.
2. Place the pan in the fryer and cook at 340°F for 20 minutes
3. Blend using an immersion blender. Divide the jam into cups and serve

Fried Bananas Recipe

(**Ready in about:** 25 Minutes | **Serves:** 4)

Ingredients:
- 3 tbsp butter
- 2 eggs
- 8 bananas; peeled and halved.
- 3 tbsp cinnamon sugar
- 1 cup panko
- ½ cup corn flour

Instructions:
1. Heat up a pan with the butter over medium high heat, add panko; stir and cook for 4 minutes and then transfer to a bowl.
2. Roll each in flour, eggs and panko mix, arrange them in your air fryer's basket, dust with cinnamon sugar and cook at 280°F, for 10 minutes. Serve right away

Made in the USA
Lexington, KY
24 March 2019